The Changing World of Work

NEW EDITION

Lesley Taylor

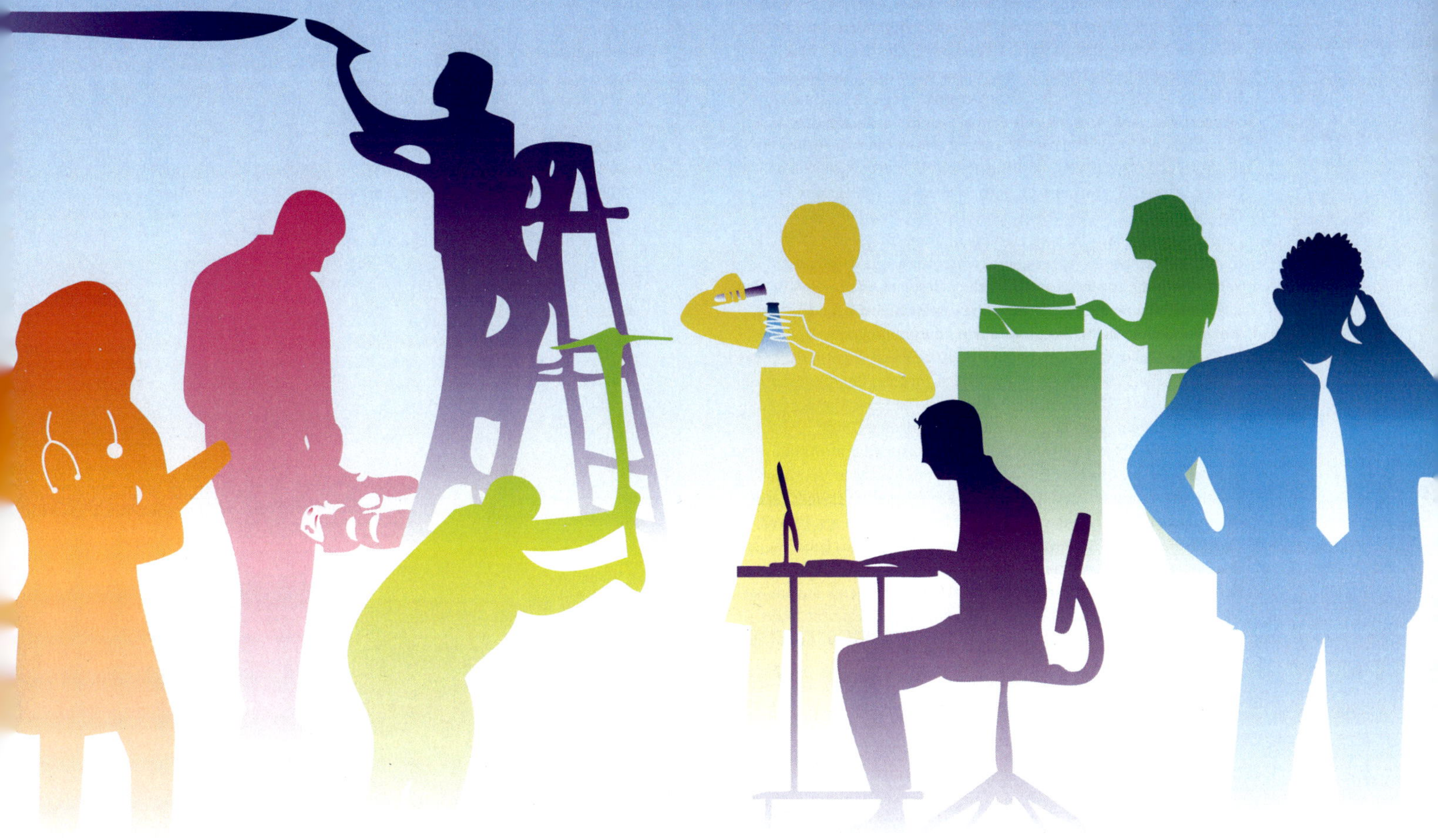

NELSON CENGAGE Learning

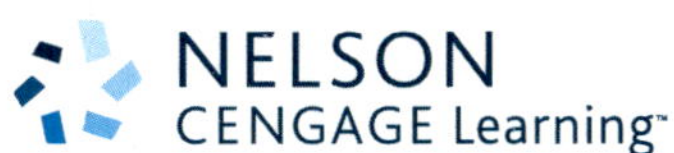

Australia • Brazil • Japan • Korea • Mexico • Singapore • Spain • United Kingdom • United States

The Changing World of Work
2nd Edition
Lesley Taylor

Designer: Macarn Design
Illustrator: Felicity Bridle

Any URLs contained in this publication were checked for currency during the production process. Note, however, that the publisher cannot vouch for the ongoing currency of URLs.

Acknowledgements
Alexander Turnbull Library, National Library of New Zealand – Page 8, (top) Goodwin, Arnold Frederick; (bottom) Boy sheep shearer [between 1910-1930s] Reference No. 1/1-006299-G Part of Northwood brothers : Photographs of Northland (PA-Group-00027). Page 9, Freelance Collection; National Publicity Studios Collection; Gordon Burt Collection; Northwood Collection; Cowles shop front, Lambton Quay, Wellington. [circa 1880]. Page 10, (top row) Evening Post Collection; Freelance Collection; NZ Freelance; Man in a vehicle, pulling trailor loads of butter, Wellington wharves Part of Smith, Sydney Charles, 1888-1972 : Photographs of New Zealand (PAColl-3082); Farmer droving sheep, Bay of Plenty [ca 1946] Reference No. PAColl-8163-83 Part of New Zealand Free Lance: Photographic prints and negatives (PA-Group-00079). Page 12, Trades Union demonstration. Wellington 1979, The Dominion Post Collection (EP/1979/1743/19A-F). **IStock** - page 13, line production; clothing store (Sean Locke); page 14, (B) Dan Moore, (C) Ame Thaysen, (E), (H) Olga, (K) Jovana Cetkovic, (L) Brent Bossam, (M) Kendall Griffin; page 19, Bulent Ince; page 22, (A) Joas Kotzsch, (B), (D) Arno Massee, (E) Don Bayley; page 23, Martin Maun; page 20 (snowboarder) Jeff Patterson; page 27, (steel) Volker Kreinacke, (hair dresser) Lian Leong, (mechanics) Chris Schmidt; page 28 (from top down) Dr Heinz Linke, Robert Kylio, Brian Goodman, Fadhil Kamarudin; page 29 (from top right down) Nicolette Neish, Chris Schmidt; page 34 (TV) Slobo Mitic, (film crew) Ulrike Mammerich; page 35 (from 2nd image down) Wolfgang Lienbacher, Nicolette Neish, Dan Driedger. **Other Images** – page 13, Frost rakers on Neudorf Vineyard - Tim and Judy Finn of Neudorf Vineyard; page 15, Taupo Tandem Skydiving; page 17, robotic arm – Manukau Technical Institute; page 18, (left) Bay of Plenty Polytechnic, (top right) Rakon, (lower) Kruse (NZ) Ltd; page 20, (left) Glidepath, (middle) Dairy farming – DairyNZ; page 22, (C) Recycling - University of Canterbury, (F) A biodigester on a dairy farm - Environment Canterbury; page 24, Pachoud Motor Yachts; page 27 (top) Explore NZ, (bottom left) Pachoud Motor Yachts; page 29 (top left) from NZ fashion designer Ana Steele's Winter Junkyard Collection 2008, photograph by Robin Smith; page 30, (top) Waipoua Guided walks, (bottom) Tamaki Tours photographs by Tony Hadlow finelinecreative; page 31, (left) Charles Royal, (right) Whale Watch Kaikoura; page 33 (left) Napier City Council, (middle) Geoff Wright from Wright Vineyard, Gisborne; page 34 (bottom) The Peter Minturn Goldsmith School; page 37, Taupo Tandem Skydiving. Other acknowledgements – Graham Taylor; Hinekahukura Barratt-Aranui; Keith Robinson, Supply Chain; N.Z. Dairy Board; Chris Raynal; Scarborough Fair, Lighthouse Ventures; Wellington Drive Technologies, Auckland; Zespri International, N.Z; Statistics N.Z; Dept of Labour; Tricia Legg, Paeroa; Koro Carmen, Footprints Waipoua; Wendy Bennett, Indigenous Food Tours; Ross Jones, Careers Service; Lauri Russell; Martyn Newby, Centracast; Future In Tech, Institution of Professional Engineers; Derek Boston, Mt Maunganui College; N.Z. Trade and Enterprise Board; Tourism News; Garry Robinson, Manukau Technical Institute; Mike Dudson, Bay of Plenty Polytechnic.

National Library of New Zealand Cataloguing-in-Publication Data
Taylor, Lesley, 1940-
The changing world of work / Lesley Taylor. 2nd ed.
Previous ed.: 1999.
ISBN 978-0-1701-8018-4
1. Labor supply—New Zealand—Juvenile literature. 2. Labor market—New Zealand—Juvenile literature. 3. Vocational guidance—New Zealand—Juvenile literature. [1. Labor market—New Zealand. 2. Vocational guidance—New Zealand.] I. Title.
331.1230993—dc 22

Cengage Learning Australia
Level 7, 80 Dorcas Street
South Melbourne, Victoria Australia 3205

Cengage Learning New Zealand
Unit 4B Rosedale Office Park
331 Rosedale Road, Albany, North Shore 0632, NZ

For learning solutions, visit **cengage.com.au**

Printed in Australia by Ligare Pty Ltd
5 6 7 8 9 10 11 20 19 18 17 16

Contents

1 Work in Earlier Times

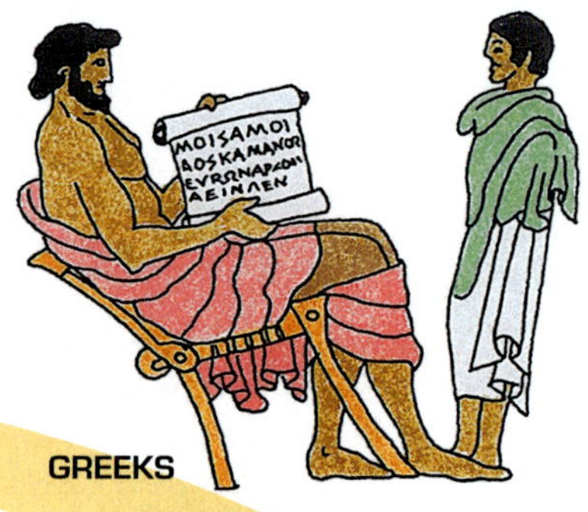

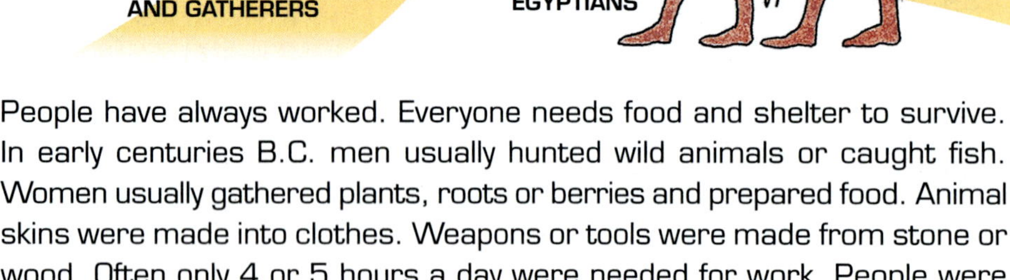

People have always worked. Everyone needs food and shelter to survive. In early centuries B.C. men usually hunted wild animals or caught fish. Women usually gathered plants, roots or berries and prepared food. Animal skins were made into clothes. Weapons or tools were made from stone or wood. Often only 4 or 5 hours a day were needed for work. People were usually **nomadic,** moving often to find new sources of food.

The Egyptians

From about 3000 B.C. to 500 B.C. the Ancient Egyptians farmed along the Nile River. They learnt how to **irrigate** and plough fields. This meant they could stay in one place instead of moving all the time. Their small villages often became large cities. Fish were caught in the Nile.

Rich Egyptians often lived in big houses made from mud bricks. Bright colours decorated the walls inside. Servants cooked, and looked after gardens and animals. Women often wove material for clothes or made rugs. Writing of letters or laws was done on **papyrus.**

Peasants grew and harvested crops. They also built boats. These were used for fishing or to trade goods with others living along the river. **Barges** may also have been used to bring stone blocks up the Nile to make the pyramids.

The Greeks and Romans

The Greeks and Romans also built great cities about this time. Beautiful buildings, **temples** and bridges were made. The Greeks were especially interested in medicine, art and athletics. The Romans worked out new laws and ways of governing people. They also built many long roads made of concrete. Some parts of these still exist today. Men from important Greek or Roman families became the rulers or priests. Rich women usually stayed home and cared for families. They were helped by slaves. Many people, both men and women, were farmers. Others owned shops or made crafts to earn money.

Language Box

nomadic: moving from place to place, never staying very long anywhere.
irrigate: provide water to crops through channels.
papyrus: material like paper made from water plants which have been flattened and dried.
peasants: farm workers, often very poor.
barges: flat-topped boats.
temples: churches.

The Agricultural Age

In England and Europe

Until about 1700 AD most people in England and Europe worked on the land. Some owned small farms, but most were serfs. **Serfs** were not paid but they did have small strips of land to grow their own vegetables. Some kept a cow or two pigs as well. Women often spun wool or grew vegetables to sell in markets. In towns **artisans** and apprentices made furniture, lace, candles or woollen materials. Some were stonemasons or wheelwrights. Families all worked together. Children usually followed their parents' **occupations**. **Aristocrats** did little work but had plenty of servants.

In Asian countries like Malaysia and Thailand

Like people in Europe and other places, many Asians worked on small farms. They grew a wide range of crops like soybeans, citrus fruits, cinnamon or sweet potatoes. Most important though were rice and tea. Fishing was a major occupation. Families kept chickens, pigs or perhaps buffalo. Trade with China and India was important too.

In the Pacific Islands

Early Centuries AD

- **Subsistence farming:** people grew vegetables, taro, coconuts, pineapples or bananas. Most kept pigs and chickens too.
- Fishing around the islands for deep-sea and lagoon fish. Shellfish were gathered.
- Traded any extra goods with nearby islands.
- Wove mats, baskets and clothes from flaxes and other plants.

Late 1700s

- Europeans helped set up coconut plantations for copra (dried coconut).
- Copra and bananas were exported to other countries.

1940 onwards

- Many Pacific Islanders moved to New Zealand. They worked in hospitals, forestry, car assembly and factories of different kinds.

Language Box

serfs: farm workers who 'belonged' to the lord of the manor.
artisans: skilled tradespeople.
occupation: job, employment.
aristocrats: lords, ladies, from noble families.
subsistence farming: families usually had to grow all their own food, often very poor.

Activities 1

1 What was the main work of men and women in very early times?
2 Why could the Egyptians settle along the Nile instead of being nomadic?
3 What was built during this period that can still be seen today? Use the Internet or a book to find a picture.
4 Apprentices are trained as they work. This takes three or four years. Apprentices in early England were like apprentices today in New Zealand.
Ask for a list of apprenticeships from your Careers Advisor or teacher.
Choose one that interests you. Write a paragraph about the sort of work they do.
5a What were two kinds of work done in both Asian countries and in the Pacific Islands?
b Give five kinds of food each area grew.
c What were the main animals they kept? Illustrate your answers.

The Industrial Age

In 1700 about 90% of people in England worked on farms. Over the next 150 years there were many changes. New inventions in **farm equipment** meant more crops could be grown. Much **common land was enclosed**. This left peasants with no land to grow their own food. Many had to find jobs in towns.

There were other inventions in spinning and weaving. Factories were built in towns. These produced mainly woollen goods till 1810. Then cotton clothes became more popular. Fewer families worked in **cottage industries**.

The new steam engine and coal mines provided power to factories. Iron was made and railways were built. There were often very bad conditions in factories however. Men, women and children often worked 10-12 hours a day. They had little rest and very low wages. This was the beginning of **mass production.**

Between 1700 -1850 England's population grew from 9 million to 28 million.

How did the changes affect people's working lives?

- Mostly outdoor farm work.
- Cottage industries and families working together.
- Self-employed peasants or partly independent serfs.
- Both men's and women's work seen as important in cottage and farm industries.
- Co-operative working together in groups and villages.
- Mainly working to provide food and clothes for own needs.
- **Varying hours** of work depending on the seasons and the work to be done.
- Use of simple tools and equipment.

- More indoor factory or mine work.
- Separation of men, women and children into different jobs.
- More people being 'employed' by others.
- Men's work for wages in factories seen as more important than women's work at home.
- Less working for the **'common good'** and more for your family or yourself.
- Mainly working to get the means (money) to buy what was needed.
- Long days, repetitive work.
- Learning to use more **complex** tools and machines.

Language Box

farm equipment: tools and machines like ploughs.
common land was enclosed: anybody could use common land but gradually farm owners or lords put fences up and kept the land for themselves.
cottage industries: whole families making lace, woollen cloth or furniture in their small cottages.
mass production: making large numbers of the same thing on machines.
varying hours: different every day.
common good: everyone in a group or a village.
complex: more complicated.

Activities

1 What were two big changes for poor farmers after 1700?
2 What were most clothes made from up until 1810?
3 Use the box below. There are 11 different inventions, all jumbled up. Make a History Road like the one on page 4, *but* arrange the inventions in the correct time order. You should start your road with 1700 and finish at 1850. Illustrate one or two inventions.

Important Inventions in England

- 1836 – first successful combine harvester
- 1790 – the spinning mule used in factories, especially for cotton
- 1813 – first publicised use of fertiliser
- 1785 – Edmund Cartwright made a power loom for weaving
- 1701 – Jethro Tull invented the horsedrawn hoe and seed drill
- 1830 – first steam-powered plough
- 1730 – the four-crop rotation system used for farming
- 1825 – first railway built – from Stockton to Darlington
- 1782 – James Watt invented the rotary steam engine
- 1801-10 – most enclosures of land were made
- 1767 – James Hargreaves' spinning jenny produced eight threads instead of one

4 Many people moved from farm work and cottage industries to factory work. What would these changes mean for many children? Write 2-3 sentences about this.
5 How would mass production of things like clothes affect cottage industries? (Clue: 'less need')
6 What was the change in the importance of men's and women's work? Do you think some women who stay home today caring for small children feel the same? Discuss in class.

2 Work in Early New Zealand

Early Maori

The early Maori tribes worked mostly as hunters and gatherers. They hunted big birds like moa. They collected shellfish like pipi and kina. They fished in the sea and caught eels in rivers and lakes. Birds were often preserved and fish were dried to use later. Fern root or aruhe was an important food. Berries were gathered and steamed. Puha and young fern tips were used as green vegetables. Tribes often shifted their homes to be near food in season.

From about the fourteenth century on, **horticulture** led to a more settled life. Kumara and many other crops were grown, mostly by the women. **Fortified** pa were built to protect crops that were harvested. Tribes planted, harvested and stored crops and other food each year in a planned way. Their **mana** was increased if they could provide big feasts for visiting tribes. In winter they had enough time to build houses or carve tools and ornaments. This was the time when women wove clothes or baskets.

Some tribes lived inland and some lived on the coast. Sometimes they exchanged food. An example would be preserved forest birds for fish caught in the sea.

Early Maori had close **spiritual** ties to nature. They practised **conservation** of animals and birds. If birds were nesting, for example, they couldn't be hunted. Maori called this **ban** a rahui.

Language Box

horticulture: gardening, especially of vegetables and fruit.
fortified: tall fences and ditches built around storehouses to prevent attack and theft by other tribes.
mana: respect shown to them, importance or influence.
spiritual: sacred, sometimes supernatural or divine.
conservation: keep or protect for use at a later time, perhaps for later generations.
ban: something that is forbidden.

Activities 3

1 Write down five different kinds of work being done in the picture.
2 Early Maori planned most of their work in a seasonal way. This means they did a certain job during the season that suited it best. Make a diagram showing the different work Maori did each season. Start with seed-sowing and planting in early spring.
3 What are two kinds of jobs that are seasonal in New Zealand today? (A web-site on 'seasonal work' might help.)
4 Find pictures of eel traps, carved ornaments, tools or spears made by early Maori. Draw them. Write one or two sentences about what they were made from or how they were used.

New Settlers

In the early 1800s many people sailed from England to live in New Zealand. By 1860 there were about 60,000 settlers here. Some Maori tribes, especially those from Waikato, Bay of Plenty and Wairarapa, grew big crops of grain around this time. They traded these around New Zealand coasts, and also across to Australia and South America. Soon, however, the settlers needed more land for cattle and sheep farms. Gradually the tribes either sold their land or had it taken away by the government to give to the settlers.

The diagram below shows some of the ways Maori were affected by English **immigration**.

What Happened Then?

- Many tribes were not left with enough land to grow crops on for themselves or for trading.
- Many Maori had to find paid jobs to live. They became farm workers, **gum-diggers**, shearers, scrub-cutters or cleaners. Jobs were often hard to find.
- The settlers brought diseases like the flu with them. Many Maori died because they had no **immunity** to these diseases.
- Early Maori lived mainly in country areas. From about 1910 on, though, many moved to towns to find jobs. Often they lost contact with their tribes.
- Metal tools, blankets and new crops like potatoes were introduced by the settlers. With new tools Maori learnt to build with wood. They were able to build bigger houses, and boats like **schooners**.

Life was hard for many settlers too. Some landowners were rich and had servants. Many people however worked 12-14 hour days. Many were farm workers. Twelve-year-old Tom was one of these:

Tom's Day

It was 5 o'clock on a freezing winter morning in 1854. Tom dressed, lit a lamp and walked across the farmyard. He chopped enough wood to keep the cook's stove going all day. Then he milked the two cows.

Breakfast for him was porridge, bread and **dripping** and hot tea. Ruth was his 14-year-old sister and she was a housemaid. Their mother was the washerwoman for the big farm house where they lived. After breakfast Tom had to shear a few sheep with hand shears. Then he was sent out to the back paddocks. He had to pick up the dead rabbits shot by the rabbiter and dump them in a hole. After that he stopped to eat his bread and cheese for lunch. Then he had to dig out thistles. As it got dark he **trudged** back home. He had to clean out the yard and feed the animals. At last he could stop for tea and fall into bed.

Activities 4

1 Why did many Maori people lose their land from about 1860 on?
2 What was one good effect of English settlement on the Maori, and one bad effect?
3 Were jobs easy to find?
4 What did **gum-diggers** do?
5 Five different kinds of jobs are mentioned. List them.
6 Many other people worked on big farms at that time too. Here are some: shepherds, coachmen, ploughmen, governesses, carters. Choose two, research what they did and write one or two sentences about each.

Language Box

immigration: coming in to a country to live.
gum-diggers: people who dug for gum. This was a sticky substance that came from kauri trees, mainly in Northland.
immunity: being able to resist something, stop it happening.
schooners: small ships with more than one mast.
dripping: fat melted by roasting meat.
trudged: walk slowly and in a tired way.

What Did Women Do?

Why do people do the jobs they do? Three possible reasons are: closeness to where they live, qualifications they have, and what kind of work is available. Other reasons include beliefs or attitudes people hold. 'A woman's place is in the home' was a common belief in the nineteenth and early twentieth centuries. In reality many women did paid work as well as being mothers and housekeepers because they needed the money.

Common jobs for women were dressmaking, nursing or infant teaching. Many were also **domestic** servants, shop assistants, clerks or typists. Pay for women was much lower than for men. In 1880, for example, a male **tailor** earned 70 shillings a week but a female tailoress only 26-35 shillings a week . By 1913 women in the **public service** were still paid much less than men. This was because some people thought women couldn't stand 'the strain of pressure that men can'! Women were also usually expected to resign from their jobs when they got married. This was so they could look after their husbands, children and homes properly.

Girls could learn typing because 'it is a class of work that does not require a tremendous amount of brains'.
(Director of Auckland Technical Institute)

An **academic education** had 'evil effects' for girls.
(two well-known doctors)

Excessive schooling led to **invalidism** in women.
(common idea)

Activities 

1. What was the belief that affected the kinds of jobs women did in the early twentieth century?
2. What percentage approximately of a male tailor's wage did a female tailoress earn?
3. Find out what the percentage difference is today for male and female pay. This will be the average for all kinds of jobs. The Department of Labour website might help you.
4. What are the two main things these quotes are saying about women? Use your own words. Your class may want to talk about these beliefs some more.
5. Look at the chart of 'Numbers of women in the paid workforce.' Draw a graph to show the increase between 1874 to 1926 more clearly.

Numbers of women in the paid workforce

1874 -	11.1%
1901 -	23%
1926 -	27%

Language Box

domestic: to do with the home, house or family.
tailor: maker of men's clothes, e.g. suits.
public service: government departments.
academic education: subjects like history or languages. These are mostly studied by learning, not by practical means or 'doing', e.g. woodwork or cooking.
invalidism: being disabled by illness or injury.

3 Changing Times, Changing Roles

During the 1930s times were hard. Many people lost their jobs in the **Depression.** The Government employed thousands of men to give them some income. They built roads and planted pine forests. Women had to work hard too. They grew food and made clothes for their families. They often worked on their farms too.

Usually though men and women did different work from each other. The man's role was to be the **breadwinner**. The woman's role was to be the wife, mother and perhaps unpaid **charity worker**.

Then from 1939-1945 the Second World War took place. Suddenly **traditional** roles began to change.

Above are some pictures from the 1930s Depression. Men working on the Government work-schemes often lived in camps. Much of the work was done by hand and was very hard. Many families became very poor and had little food. Some people went on protest marches. There were a few fights as police tried to stop the marches.

Language Box

Depression: a long period of 5-6 years in the early 1930s when the economy collapsed. Many jobs were lost.

breadwinner: the person who earned the money for a family to live on.

charity worker: someone who worked as a volunteer for organisations, with no pay.

traditional: ways of doing things over many generations.

active service: joining the Armed Forces to go and fight.

essential work: work that really has to be done, e.g. keeping the electricity running, supplying the soldiers' needs, feeding the farm animals.

DURING AND AFTER THE WAR

Young men unfit for **active service** had to do **essential work** in factories and mills. Older retired men often worked with them.

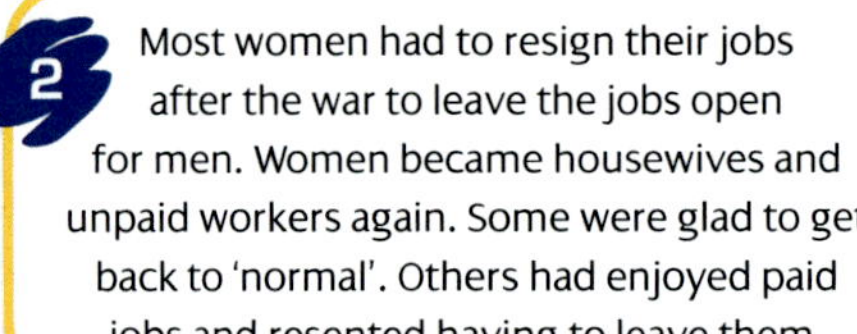

Most women had to resign their jobs after the war to leave the jobs open for men. Women became housewives and unpaid workers again. Some were glad to get back to 'normal'. Others had enjoyed paid jobs and resented having to leave them.

Fit young women had to leave home to do essential work too. They worked in factories making shoes, soldiers' clothes and helmets and many other things.

Young men left farms, factories, shops and offices to join the armed forces and fight overseas.

When the war ended there were victory celebrations everywhere.

Huge numbers of older women formed committees or groups to support New Zealand soldiers. They knitted hats and socks, collected food parcels or made up sewing kits.

Many single women stayed on in paid jobs after the war. The biggest group were in clerical and typing jobs.

Some young women joined the WWSA (Women's War Services Auxiliary). They became truck drivers or secretaries. Some went overseas with the armed forces as nurses.

Average weekly wages in 1945 were 5.5 pounds (approx $11) for men, and 3.3 pounds (approx $7) for women. Women couldn't get apprenticeships except for hairdressing.

Some young women became 'land girls' on farms. They replaced male farmers or farm workers who had left to become soldiers.

When men returned from war many went back to their old jobs. The Government helped others to do some training, e.g. at university. Some were helped to buy farms.

New Zealand farms did very well after the war. Britain needed all the meat and dairy foods we could produce.

Activities 

1 The statements in the boxes (page 10) and pictures (below) have been muddled up. See if you can match each statement with the correct picture. Start with 1 and finish at 12, for example you might have 1-A (not correct).

2 Six of the statements are about what happened during the 1939-45 War.

- **a** List the numbers of these statements.
- **b** What three groups of people had to do the 'essential work' in New Zealand during the War?
- **c** Do some research on the 1939-45 War. Make a poster or collage that shows what fighting in the Armed Services meant. You will need to include the Army, Navy and Air Force. Find out approximately how many New Zealanders were killed overseas.

3 After the War the work of many men and women changed. Look at the six statements describing this and answer these questions.

- **a** What happened to many returning soldiers?
- **b** What happened to many women who had done the men's jobs while they were away?

PICTURES OF DURING AND AFTER THE WAR

A

B

C

D

E
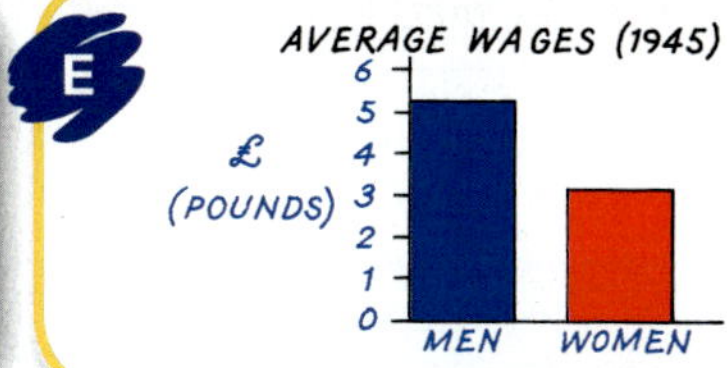

F

G

H

I

J

K

L

Restructuring

For 25 years after the Second World War New Zealand had almost full employment. This means that most people who wanted jobs could find them.

From the 1970s on, however, things changed. England and other Western countries were having problems financially. They couldn't afford as much of our farm produce as before. Our businesses weren't doing very well either. They had to **lay off** many staff. Unemployment began to rise. At the same time more women were joining the work force.

Up until the 1980s the Government owned big employers like the railways, airports, post-office, radio and TV, and gas and electricity services. During the 1980s and 1990s however, most of these were sold to private companies. They ran them like businesses and many more people lost their jobs.

Many manufacturing businesses also suffered when the Government stopped helping them financially. They did this to help the New Zealand economy to grow and develop. At the time, however, even more workers lost their jobs. Unemployment rose very quickly. This whole process was called restructuring.

Language Box

lay off: to fire from a job.
traditionally female: always been seen as suited for women.
equal opportunities: the argument that women should be able to do any job they wanted.
supplement: to add to in order to improve.
discriminate: to see a difference between things or people, sometimes unfairly. At this time women were discriminated against so that they were not allowed to do what were seen as traditionally male jobs e.g. electrician, engineer.

Women in the Workforce 1970s -1990s

During the 1970s and 1980s New Zealand, like other countries, had a big increase in certain jobs. Many of these jobs were **traditionally female** ones, for example in retail, clerical and tourism.

Sometimes one family income was not enough. Women often worked part-time to **supplement** the man's income.

More women also began working full-time, e.g. as teachers. Many had families as well. Some had to provide the only family income.

Much unpaid work, for example in playcentres, provided good training. This was a helpful stepping-stone to getting paid jobs.

Numbers of women in the workforce rose quickly. Women made up 25% of the paid workforce in 1961 but over 44% in 1996.

Not many women were in management jobs, apart from teachers and nurses. In 1982, for example, there were only three female bank managers.

The Government passed two Acts which helped women working. The 1972 Equal Pay Act meant that at last women doing the same jobs as men were paid the same. The 1978 Human Rights Commission Act made it illegal to **discriminate** against women in the workplace.

In spite of this, however, women still faced discrimination in several jobs. Working towards '**equal opportunities**' in paid jobs became a big issue in the 1980s.

Activities 7

1 Find one reason in the restructuring section (above) why many people lost their jobs in the 1980s especially.

2 Using the graph below, find the approximate difference in numbers unemployed between 1975 and 1992.

3 What happened in 2000? Give the approximate numbers of unemployed people then.

4 Using the 'Women in the Workforce' diagram answer these questions:

a Why did many women join the paid workforce at this time? Give one reason.

b What was the problem facing some girls and women who wanted 'different' sorts of jobs?

c This was a difficult time for many men too. Some jobs were seen as 'unsuitable' for women. Some objected to women being paid the same, or perhaps 'taking' their jobs. Your parents or grandparents might remember these issues. Do some research, and then discuss it in groups of four. Report back to the class.

Changing Kinds of Jobs

Approximately 2,072,900 people had paid jobs in New Zealand in December 2005. All kinds of jobs were included but they can be divided into three groups. These are: primary, secondary and tertiary. Sometimes the tertiary group is called the service **sector**.

People employed in the primary sector work in farming or horticulture. They may also work in forestry, fishing or mining. They produce 'raw materials'. Examples might be milk from dairy farms, or fruit and flowers from orchards or greenhouses. Forestry workers produce logs and miners dig out coal or gold.

In the secondary sector people make or manufacture these raw materials into other goods. Milk, for example is made into cheese or ice cream. Logs are turned into furniture or planks to build houses. Other kinds of jobs are also included in this sector. They are building and construction jobs, and jobs in the electricity, gas and water **industries**.

The **tertiary** or service sector is very wide. These jobs are not usually about producing goods. Instead people provide a skill or service that others need. Service sector jobs might be in tourism, health, education, law, **retail**, banking, transport or **IT.**

Since about 1950 many more people have been employed in service sector jobs. Fewer people have been employed in the other two sectors. The chart below shows the approximate percentage of the workforce in each sector 1951-2005.

Employment in each sector, 1951–2005

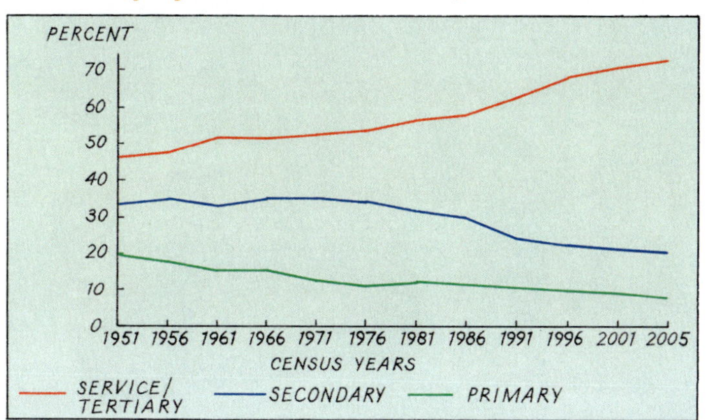

Primary and Secondary jobs

carpenter	coalminer
mussel farmer	forester
scaffolder	aircraft engineer
electrician	power plant operator
flower grower	ostrich farmer
farm manager	cheese maker
timber processing worker	concrete worker
apricot grower	apple picker
oyster farm worker	onion grower
plastics machine operator	electronic engineer

Language Box

sector: a large part or group, a section of the whole.
industries: particular group of businesses doing the same kind of work e.g. electricity businesses.
tertiary: third.
retail: businesses selling things to the public, shops.
IT: Information Technology, covering all kinds of computer-oriented businesses.

Activities 8

1 Study the 'Primary and Secondary jobs' list. Draw up two columns and put the jobs into the correct column. Read the information on the page carefully first.

2 Look at the graph called 'Employment in each sector'. Describe the trend for each of the three sectors between 1951 and 2005. Include the approximate movement in percentage terms between the two dates, e.g. from 10% to 20%.

3 Can you present this graph information in a different way? Some of you may like to draw a bar graph using say 1966, 1986 and 2005. Others of you may want to present the major trends differently.

Why are the Sectors Changing?

There are two main causes of change: new technology and increasing competition. *New technology* means things can be done often much faster, and with fewer people. *Increased competition* means New Zealand farms and things we make and do now have to compete with similar things all over the world. They have to be better, or cheaper, or perhaps different if we want to sell them. For example:

Language Box

robotic technology: computerised machinery that automatically does tasks usually done by a person, eg. put tops on bottles in a soft drink factory.
wholesale: selling large amounts of things, usually from a factory or warehouse, not selling through shops.
accommodation: places where visitors stay for one or more nights.

Primary sector

1 The prices for sheep meat and wool have been low for many years. Many smaller farms have been combined into one big farm. This is called 'consolidation'. There are now fewer farm owners and farm labourers than there were.
2 Between 1985 and 2005 dairy production increased by 85%, but the numbers of people working in dairy factories went up only by 1000 – from 8,600 to 9,600. Numbers in meat processing dropped from 39,000 to 30,000.
3 Quad bikes save time on farms. So do conveyor belt systems used by vets. They can vaccinate 1000 sheep an hour. This used to take two people 1-2 days!

Secondary sector

4 Computerised machinery and **robotic technology** now take the place of hundreds of workers. They are also much faster and can work all day, all night and on public holidays.
5 There is mass production of goods, especially from Asian countries where wages are low. Things like clothes, electronic goods and cell phones can be made much cheaper there than they can here.

Service sector

6 More things to buy and more tourists mean more sales assistants in shops and more workers in cafes, hotels, planes and so on. Selling **wholesale** or retail employed the biggest group of people in New Zealand in 2004: 354,200.
7 More and more people work with information. They use words, numbers, ideas or design. Computers can find and make more and more information, faster and faster! Workers have to learn new things every day. Scientists research and test information out, librarians store it, you learn it and so on!
8 One of the biggest and fastest growing parts of the service sector concerns working closely with people. Health, education, tourism, entertainment and recreation employ many thousands of people.

Activities 9

Study the pictures of service sector jobs below:-
a List the jobs you think each one is about.
b Why are these jobs different from primary and secondary sector ones? (You may need to read page 13 again.)

The Service Sector – People and Information

While almost all jobs in the service sector need people who are good at dealing with other people, many jobs focus as well on information. This information can be to do with words, numbers or ideas, or even with design or music. Some people re-organise information in new ways, for example accountants, advertisers or computer software writers.

Emma's Story

It was Emma's fourth week at the Tourist Office. The first three weeks had been spent training. She had been shown how to arrange bookings on bus trips, sky-diving adventures and loads of other things. Then she'd had to find out about hotels, motels, backpackers and other **accommodation**. There were so many leaflets, maps and so on to know about. It had been a tough three weeks.

Now here she was trying to answer the questions of two Japanese women. They wanted to know the best places to have a spa and massage. At least she thought that was what they wanted. Their English was not very good. She wished she had done more than one year of Japanese at school. And where were those leaflets? She needed help but the other staff were busy at present. She tried to explain this to the two tourists. By now there were two more in the queue behind them.

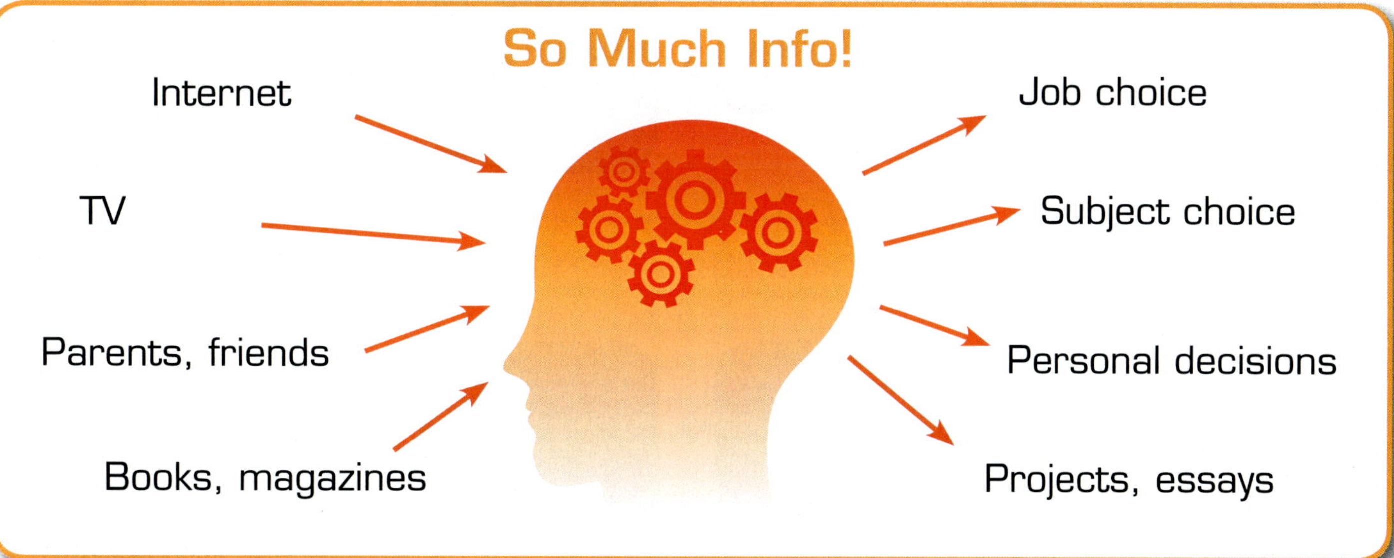

Activities 10

1 Using the information on the opposite page, write down the two main reasons for sector change. Give one example of each in the secondary sector.

2 Where do a lot of our clothes and cell phones come from?

3 To work in the service sector you need very good 'people skills'. Read Emma's story, then in groups of four, make a list of five 'people' skills you think Emma will need. Share this with the class.

4 *Mr Shelf*, *Shipshape Dog Grooming* and *Cleantastic* are three businesses offering some kind of personal service.
   a What do you think they do?
   b Find three more with catchy names! Draw a poster illustrating their jobs.

5 Using the cartoon 'So Much info!':
   a Write down three other sources of information you use fairly regularly.
   b Talk to an adult friend or family members about dealing with information in their job. Do they have to deal with new information regularly? How often? Where does it come from? How does it affect their job? Do they enjoy this or find it stressful? Prepare a five minute presentation for the class on your findings. Use PowerPoint, a poster or any other method you like.

5 Changing Technology

Over the last two or three decades new technology has given us computers and **access** to masses of new information. But even more amazing are the tiny computerised micro-chips found in just about everything else we use. Cars, phones, washing machines, iPods and so on all have them. They've changed the way we live and the way we work.

Language Box

access: a way in, a way to obtain something.

We are moving from this … → **… to this.**

Jobs needing strength like lifting logs or wool bales or digging out new roads.

Routine jobs like putting lids on bottles in a factory all day.

Manual work using our 'hands'. → Computerised work using our 'brains'.

Using computers to operate big road or forestry machines or to design quicker ways of doing these things.

Operating and adjusting robotic equipment that fills up bottles and puts the lids and labels on automatically.

Lots of workers needed to make a car or weave a carpet.

Lots of time needed to sew a dress, print a newspaper or add up rows of figures.

Most people making things. → Few people making things, more people researching and designing them.

People researching, designing and advertising new products and services, and sorting out legal or accounting problems.

Distributing and selling products in shops, feeding people in restaurants, educating, healing and entertaining them.

Leaving school at 15-16.

Some training on the job in apprenticeships. Many straight into jobs from school, a few going to university or polytechnics.

Most people needing fewer skills and lower education levels. → Most people needing high level skills and longer education.

Tertiary qualifications before employment, re-training off and on throughout life.

High levels of computer, technical, thinking, number and verbal skills needed, plus 'working with people' skills.

Activities 11

1 Using the diagram above give two examples of jobs that were once done by hand, but are now done by computerised machines or equipment.

2 Apprenticeships are still very important and are called 'tertiary qualifications' too. Find out from an older person or from written information about how life for an apprentice today is different from 30-40 years ago. Write a paragraph about this.

3 The 'Then and Now' chart shows some jobs which have almost disappeared, and some that are fairly new. Pick out two new jobs. Find out from your school Careers room what these people do and what qualifications you will need to do them.

THEN AND NOW!

Old Jobs	New Jobs
typist	network technician
telephone operator	legal executive
newspaper typesetter	dental hygienist
lift attendant	customer services assistant
radio assembler	personal trainer
tram conductor	web site developer
telegram deliverer	food technologist
glove maker	marketing manager
milkman	genetic researcher
general labourer	computer games developer
car assembler	environmental engineer

Computers again

Most jobs have been affected by computer technology in some way or other. Three types of work that are changing in amazing ways are:

Office work
Manufacturing
Retail and advertising jobs.

The first two of these illustrate the trend to computerise jobs once done by hand. Secretaries and clerical workers used to file papers, calculate figures, type, deliver information and so on. Computers now do most of these things. Receptionists are now often **office administrators** as well as many other things. Like bank tellers, they are **multi-taskers.** And the new P.A.s, or personal assistants, who work directly for top managers, often have degrees or other good qualifications.

Computerised machines now do a huge amount of work in manufacturing too. Some factories may have only one or two workers involved with actually making things. These people **monitor** and sometimes adjust the machines that are busy making taps, cellphones, microwaves, videos, cars and so on. Robotic machinery of all kinds is very common.

Major changes to retail and advertising are probably only just beginning to alter jobs. And the cause of change is of course the Internet. Some people have called this trend 'Power to the People'. Why? Because instead of using others to sell us goods, organise things like a trip overseas or sell a house we are researching and doing it ourselves on the Internet.

Look at the octopus below. It shows some of the things we now do, instead of paying other people to do them for us. Some of the businesses being affected by this trend are shown in brackets.

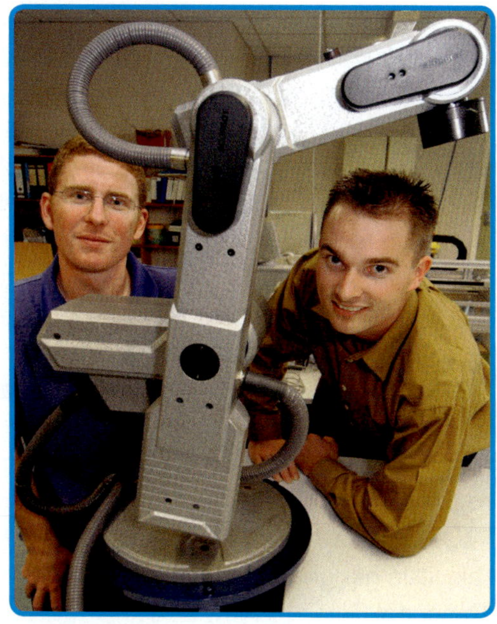

Robotic arm, Manukau Technical Institute.

Language Box

office administrator: someone who organises and manages many of the activities in an office.
multi-taskers: people who do several quite different tasks as part of their job.
monitor: watch over, make sure something works properly.

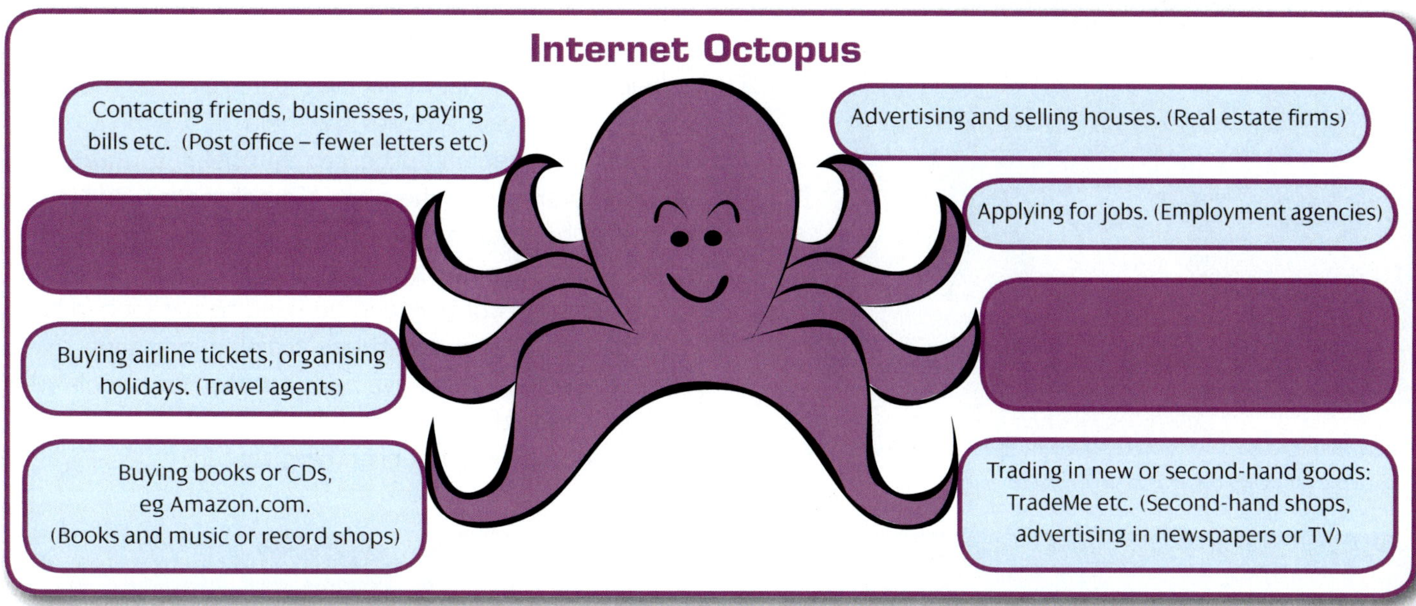

Activities 12

1 On this page we can see how some 'middle' types of jobs are changing. We can now buy airline tickets or books without going into shops. We can find a job, advertise or sell things directly.
   a Suggest two other things now done on the Internet that will probably affect traditional kinds of jobs.
   b The octopus may need eight more legs over the next few years. See if you can imagine two other jobs or work tasks that could be done over the Internet soon.

2 a What is your favourite computerised object?
   b Think about what you use it for. Before it was invented, how would you have done what it now does?

New technology doesn't just mean the obvious things we see all around us like cellphones, laptops, game-boxes and so on. There is a huge range of new technologies being developed. Many of these are creating quite NEW jobs.

In Auckland for example a company called Rakon has made a tiny radio signal receiver – probably the smallest in the world. This will be used in G.P.S. **devices**. GPS is short for Global Positioning System, a new technology which uses satellites in space to direct radio signals all over the world. It can tell you where you are if you get lost too – for example a sailor lost at sea. Rakon already make **intricate** crystals which are used in GPS devices. Now their tiny radio receiver will mean that things like cell-phones or pocket computers using GPS technology can be made very much smaller.

Rakon's radio signal receiver.

Developed by a company called Kruse in Auckland, this little gadget is another world-first. It gives people a 'Personal Guide to New Zealand'. Every 10-15 minutes it uses GPS to explain things to tourists travelling around New Zealand in rental cars. It can use many different languages. Tourists are told where they are, and a little about the history, landmarks, birds and so on that they will see as they drive past.

Kruse's personal travel guide.

Anyone involved in high level sport these days is probably using new kinds of technology too. All kinds of computer programs and **sophisticated** equipment are being used to help sports people improve. Our top swimmers for example are coached with the help of 'Silicon Coach'. This is a New Zealand program that helps to **analyse** a swimmer's stroke in the pool. 'Gamebreaker' and other programs help teams like rugby, netball or hockey. They show how team players work together, pass the ball and so on. Some programs can be used by a coach in New Zealand to monitor an athlete training overseas. New jobs in sports science have been created for people who develop or use this technology. In the photo the person exercising is having his breathing tested.

Measuring breathing patterns in performance sport.

Activities 13

1 There are thousands of new technologies besides the ones described on this page. They are being invented all the time, all over the world. What sort of skills do you think are needed to think up new technologies?

2 Most of these new technologies were not around five years ago. Choose something you use, for example an iPod or something a bit different. Now draw a flow chart or some other diagram showing how it might change over the next five years. What else might it do?

3 GPS is a very important new technology, and is used in many ways. Using the Internet or other means of research, find out two or three other uses for it. Illustrate these in a poster or in a PowerPoint presentation.

Language Box

devices: gadgets, inventions or tools.

intricate: complicated, often quite delicate.

sophisticated: complex, highly developed.

analyse: examine something in detail.

ICT stands for Information and Communication Technology. ICT is a huge part of work today. Why? Well, almost all work involves - at some stage – talking, writing or communicating with others in some way. Communication might also include pictures, numbers, music or design. Often it means sending or receiving information of some sort.

The ICT Revolution

ICT

Work

Recreation

Sometimes work, sometimes recreation

Keith Robinson runs a company called Supply Chain. He organises the delivery of all kinds of products from manufacturers to shops all over New Zealand. He uses a 'Harrier' – an electronic diary, calculator and phone. It takes emails and Internet while he is travelling. It also links to his laptop and database at his home. Wireless broadband makes communicating quick and easy.

Fast broadband is used by networks of science researchers throughout New Zealand and the world. Many also use Skype Internet phones.

University students use 'tablet' laptops. These can turn writing into typewritten notes. Voice software can turn someone's spoken words into written text.

New wireless technology that, for example, makes it possible for Team NZ sailors to talk to each other while racing. They can also talk to their shore base.

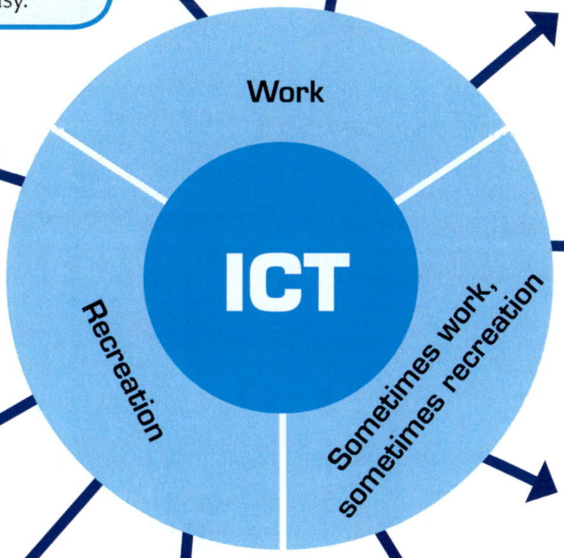

Cellphones are used to talk to customers or to friends.

Computer games often played with people in other countries - Xbox and PlayStation.

Photos and 'streaming' video on cellphones. Used for fun, but also sometimes sent to TV newsrooms to show car chases or tsunamis in real time.

Mp3 players like iPods to download the music you like.

Internet downloading of films, TV programmes and so on to watch later at home.

Screens are getting bigger and bigger. Used in homes for TV, DVDs etc. Also used at work to video-conference with others in different cities or countries.

Activities 14

1 Much new technology is said to be 'interactive'. What does that mean? Usually it means that after we do something, eg texting or pressing a button on the photo machine, we get something back like a message, information or a picture. The most common way to interact is by talking with someone. A lot of new technologies, however, make us interact by reading, listening or touching keyboards or screens.

a Using the diagram above write a list of five interactive examples of technology where actual talking is not needed.

b Think about technology you use to interact with friends or family. Do things sometimes get confused? Give an example.

c Look at the 'Work' group. What do you think the Harrier, laptops and so on mean for ***where*** you might work?

6 Changing with the World

New technology like the Internet is used world-wide for work of all kinds. Like people in other countries, New Zealanders are using new technology more and more to connect to overseas businesses.

There are cheaper and more frequent air flights now than there once were. People and products can move around the world faster and more often.

More people world wide want to visit New Zealand They want to see our beautiful scenery. They also want to learn more about our Maori culture. Often they hear about these things on the Internet or TV.

Many more countries like China, India, Korea, Thailand, Chile and others produce large amounts of goods. They compete with countries like New Zealand to sell them world-wide. Wages are usually lower in these countries than in New Zealand. This means they can often sell what they make more cheaply than New Zealand can.

New Zealand: LINKING UP GLOBALLY

About 60% of New Zealand's exports come from farms, orchards and pine forests. We can now fly cheese, meat, kiwifruit or flowers quickly all around the world to sell.

Big New Zealand manufacturing businesses can't sell everything they make here. They have to export. That means they have to make what people in the U.S., Japan or China want. They also have to be clever and think up new and different things to make and sell.

There are many very small New Zealand businesses, often run by only one or two people. They too, sometimes sell things globally.

One of New Zealand's biggest businesses is tourism. It gets bigger each year as more tourists come for holidays here. That means there are more jobs in cafes and hotels. There are also more in activities like skiing, fishing, kayaking, or organising tours to see things like Mt Cook or Rotorua's geysers.

Glidepath is a big New Zealand firm that exports to over 30 countries. They make the **automated** moving tracks that are used at airports to carry passengers' luggage around. They make some of their tracks in Texas in USA. Some of their **employees** work in offices in Sydney, Beijing, Toronto or other countries as well as in New Zealand.

In 2006 NZ had about 11,600 dairy farmers. Milk is turned into many different products. Butter, cheese and ice cream are three of the most important. Fonterra factories make lots of these products. They export them to over 40 countries. About 20% of all the money New Zealand gets from exporting things comes from dairy products.

Chris Raynal is an accountant in Auckland. He is an expert in taxation, especially for people buying or selling properties. He advertises through the Yellow Pages Internet. He also has his own website. Over half his clients live overseas and he may never meet them! He works using emails and faxes. He is also training an accountant in the Philippines using MSN Messenger, Skype and email. Chris has plenty of work and employs two or three people.

Scarborough Fair is a tiny company that makes tea, coffee bags and chocolate. It was begun by a young woman called Sarah Scarborough. Its tea and coffee are fair-trade products. That means the people in poorer countries like Sri Lanka or Panama who grow the tea and coffee are paid a 'fair' price. Usually growers are not paid very much at all. Sarah's teas and coffees are now sold in big supermarkets in New Zealand and Australia. They will soon be exported to other countries too.

Language Box

automated: controlled by a machine or computer, not run by people.
employees: those who work for an employer or owner of a business.

Activities 15

1 Why can't the people of New Zealand buy everything our manufacturers make?
2 The diagram on page 20 gives some of the **reasons** New Zealand is becoming more connected to countries in the rest of the world. Some of the **results** of this linking up are shown too. These are all shown in a kind of flow diagram. See if you can draw this diagram in another way. Perhaps you could link each reason more directly with one or more of the results. For example more air travel helps our exports of fruit. You may want to add in other information.
3 Do some research in your town or city. Find one other business that exports something to another country. What do they send? Where does it go?

Many things are happening in the world that affect how we work. They also affect what we work at. Some of these things are called **trends.** Below you will see examples of trends that are changing jobs world-wide.

Telling Trends	
Popular electronic products like cell phones and computerised gadgets are getting smaller and cheaper all the time.	New Zealand is very isolated geographically. Australia is the only big country nearby. This sometimes makes it hard to export things. The Internet and more frequent air travel are gradually making it easier to send products and services overseas.
New Zealand's workforce is becoming more **multi-cultural**. This is seen in Auckland especially. Many different Asian and Pacific Island people live and work there. So do South Africans, English and others. Wellington Drive Technologies in Auckland for example, use multi-cultural staff to communicate in over 9 languages with customers world-wide. They make high-tech electronic motors for appliance manufacturers. These motors are 'electricity saving'; that is they use much less electricity than other motors. Good language and cultural skills are vital for the firm to succeed.	Finding new sources of energy, and using energy more efficiently is providing many new jobs. A lot of work is going into saving energy – efficient light bulbs for example. How else can we save energy? And how can we make milk or metal products using coal or oil-fired energy without spilling out dirty waste into the air? How do we use renewable hydro power without spoiling our rivers and lakes? Wind and solar power are part of the answer. But what about making power from dairy farms' effluent? Plenty of questions – we need the answers.
The number of women in paid work is increasing all the time. Many are mainly responsible for caring for their children too.	China, India and other countries are big markets for us. However not many New Zealanders speak other languages or understand other cultures. Sometimes this causes problems when we try to sell them our products.
More and more people suffer from obesity. Other diseases like diabetes are also increasing. Eating too much or eating the wrong food contribute to these problems.	Creative people are developing new technologies, new gadgets and new inventions more and more often. They influence how we work and the games we play.
People are living and working more in foreign countries. About 20% of New Zealanders work in other countries. Some stay only two or three years, others stay much longer.	More people are concerned about recycling and environmental things. Many try to avoid using products with chemicals in them that could have bad effects. There is a growing market for safe food, cleaning products or things like hair shampoos.
In big cities worldwide, traffic pollution and traffic jams are major problems. They are getting worse.	More teenagers all round the world are following similar fashion trends. They also often listen to the same music over the Internet, TV or MP3 players.
As people get busier, they want quick meals to prepare. They eat out more or want meals delivered.	Over the last two or three **decades** fewer babies have been born in Western countries. That means there are fewer young workers in the workforce. More people in their 50s and 60s are staying in work rather than retiring.
More and more people are setting up small businesses on their own. They might see a 'gap' in the market, eg designing snowboarding clothing or paua jewellery.	There are very large numbers of people aged between 50-60 worldwide. They are often called **baby boomers**. There are big opportunities to make products to keep them healthy and fit.
More people are working from home than 10 or 20 years ago. They connect electronically with workmates or clients.	Many manual or labouring jobs have disappeared. Robotic machinery and computers have replaced them. The jobs that are available often need people with more skills and education.

The New Zealand Kiwifruit Board found a niche market when their research showed them that most Asian people liked sweeter-tasting kiwifruit than our green ones. They developed the yellow kiwifruit especially for them.

Language Box

trend: general direction that something is moving in.
multi-cultural: people from several different countries and cultures mixed together.
decade: one decade is 10 years.
baby boomers: large numbers of people born after the Second World War, about 1946-1964.

Activities 16

1 Pick out three trends from the chart on page 21 that interest you. Answer these questions:
   a Name two kinds of new jobs that might develop as a result of each trend. For example more women in paid work has meant new jobs for nannies to care for their children.
   b There are three or four trends that affect teenagers especially. Pick one and describe how it affects your life now. You could do this in a poster, cartoon or words.

2 What six trends are shown in the photographs at the right?

3 Find the 10 words hidden in this puzzle. The words come from the trend boxes on page 21. The first letter of each word is given below:

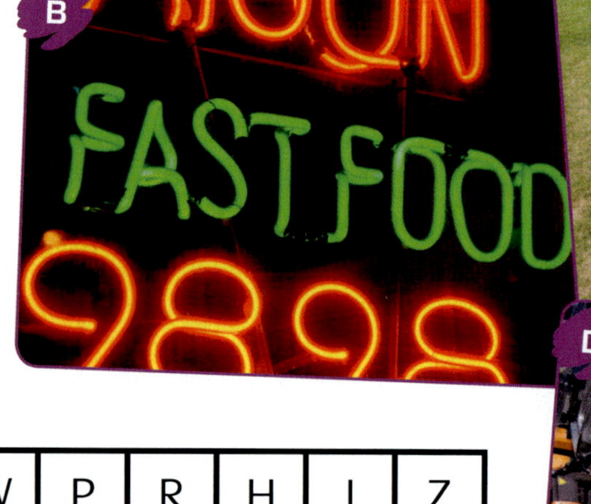

Trend 1 – g
Trend 2 – i
Trend 3 – h
Trend 4 – a
Trend 5 – w
Trend 6 – s
Trend 7 – f
Trend 8 – w
Trend 9 – f
Trend 10 – m

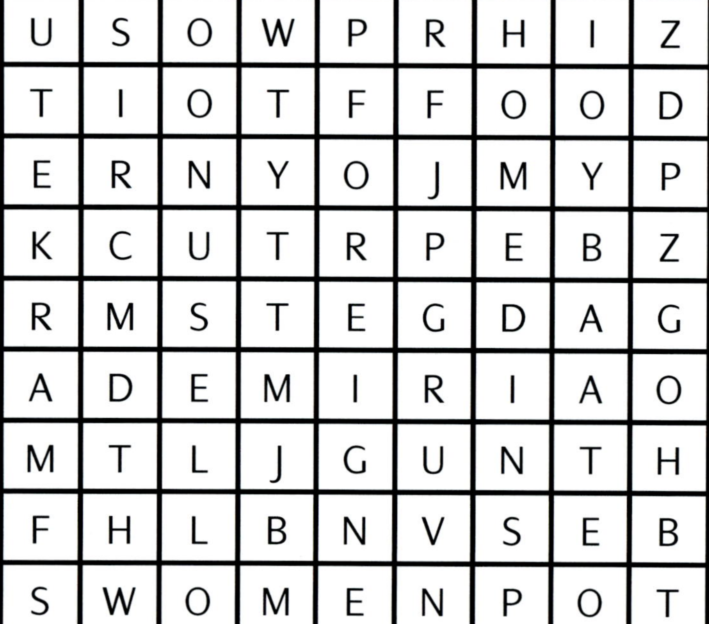

U	S	O	W	P	R	H	I	Z
T	I	O	T	F	F	O	O	D
E	R	N	Y	O	J	M	Y	P
K	C	U	T	R	P	E	B	Z
R	M	S	T	E	G	D	A	G
A	D	E	M	I	R	I	A	O
M	T	L	J	G	U	N	T	H
F	H	L	B	N	V	S	E	B
S	W	O	M	E	N	P	O	T

New Zealand is closely linked to the rest of the world in many ways. In fact all countries are becoming linked to each other more and more. The Internet, email and cellphones make this much easier to do. This is part of a trend called **globalisation**. For example, when oil prices rise in Iran or Saudi Arabia our petrol gets more expensive here. Often these things create new jobs. In this case for example some people are starting to research new kinds of fuel so we don't need to import as much petrol.

Good and Bad News

Getting closer to other countries is good news in many ways. But it can also create a few challenges for us. Here are three of them:

1 Every day we watch TV, DVDs or movies. The **majority** of these show American culture. A lot of the music we listen to and the computer games we play come from America too. In other words we often see and hear more about Americans – and people from other countries – than of people from our own country! Some people worry that New Zealand culture may gradually disappear. Our history, our music and art, and the way we speak are **unique** to New Zealand. They also employ many people. Is it important to hang on to our culture?

2 People from all over the world move to other countries for better job opportunities. New Zealanders go overseas and people from other places come here. For example many highly qualified people from Asian countries like China, Korea and India are settling here. So are people from England, Europe, Canada and so on. Jobs in New Zealand are better paid for some of them. Others like the space and lifestyle New Zealanders enjoy! We need their job-skills and new ideas, but some people think that too many people from other countries are settling here.

3 New Zealand advertises itself as 'clean and green'. That means we tell countries that our meat, dairy products, crops and fish are grown in an unpolluted environment. We tell tourists coming here that our water and air are clean. Like other countries, however, we're finding it hard to keep the countryside and wildlife healthy and not **polluted**. We have to control pests and look after **endangered species** like the kiwi. Many people have jobs working on **sustainability** of resources like water, forests and native birds.

Language Box

globalisation: increasingly closer links between all countries of the world.
majority: the larger amount or greater number of something.
unique: the only one of its kind.
polluted: made dirty or not pure, e.g. water mixed with chemicals or rubbish from a factory.
endangered species: animals or birds that are dying out.
sustainability: keeping something going for the future, preserving, e.g. making sure forests aren't killed by possums.

Activities 17

1 a Why are petrol prices rising in New Zealand?
b What is often the result of new trends overseas?
c What do we call the big trend that results in all countries being more closely linked?

2 This page deals with three challenges for New Zealand. Two of them talk about what some people see as too much or too many of something coming to New Zealand. What are these two things?

3 Find the latest Census results on the Internet; www.stats.govt.nz might be a good place to start. See if you can find out what percentage of the New Zealand population see themselves as Asian, Pacific Islanders, etc. Draw a graph illustrating this.

4 Do a web-search, using words and phrases like sustainability, pollution, dairy effluent and conservation in New Zealand. Now draw a diagram or poster giving an example of something you've found. Show the problem, what is being done about it, and what sorts of jobs are involved.

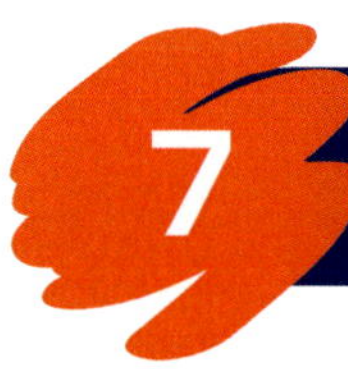

7 Changing Patterns of Working

Fifty or sixty years ago the pattern of life for most employed people, men especially, was something like this:

Leave school at 15-16
Either straight into job
Perhaps 1-2 job changes
Retire at 60
Jobs easy to find
or train for 3-4 years

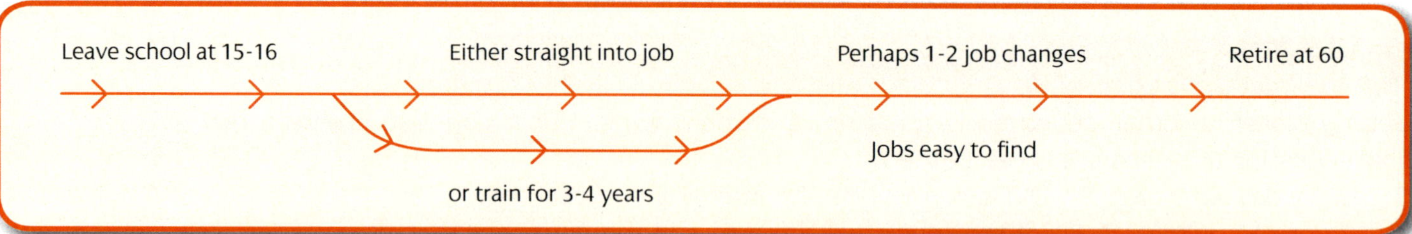

These days your pattern of work when you first leave school might look more like this:

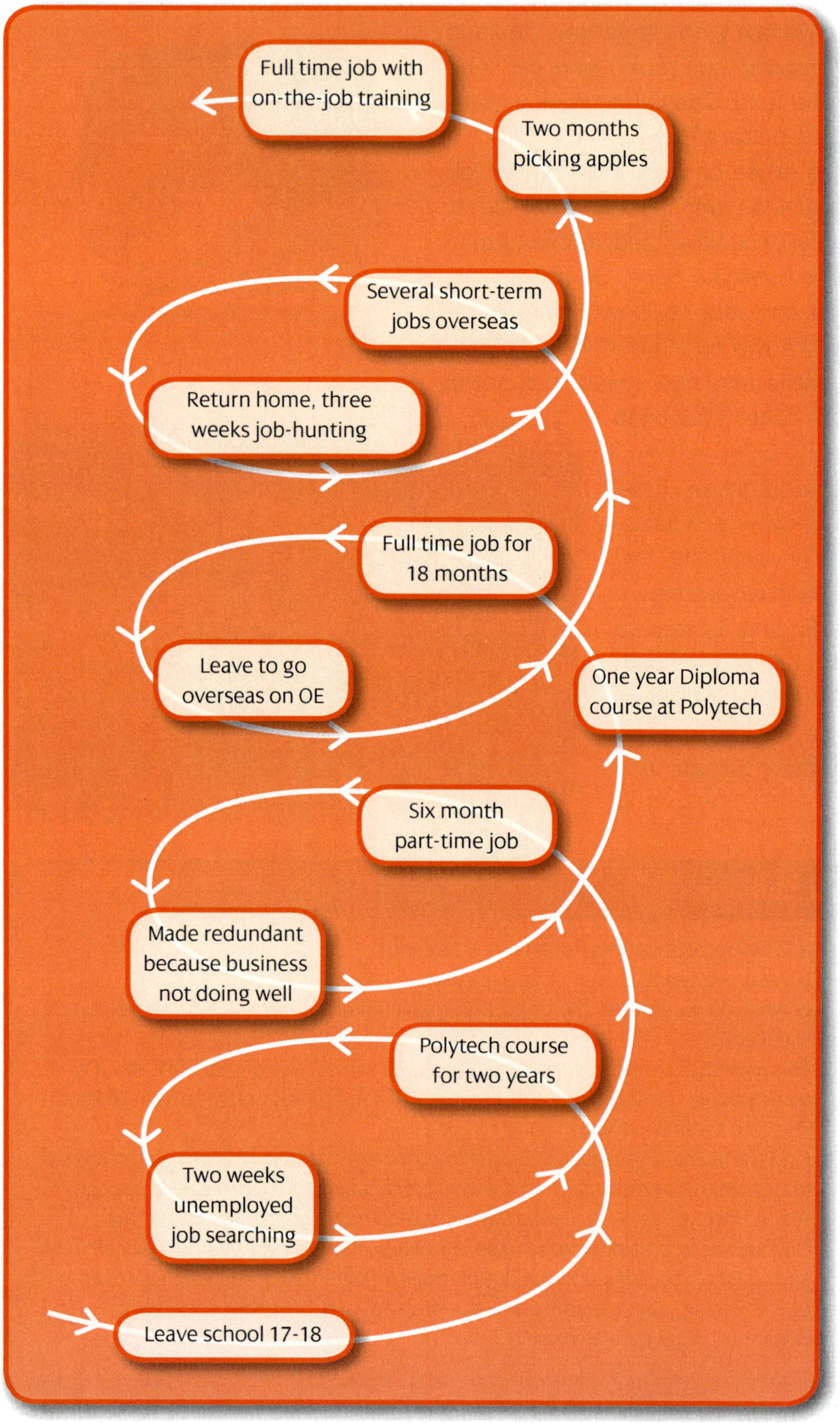

Full time job with on-the-job training
Two months picking apples
Several short-term jobs overseas
Return home, three weeks job-hunting
Full time job for 18 months
Leave to go overseas on OE
One year Diploma course at Polytech
Six month part-time job
Made redundant because business not doing well
Polytech course for two years
Two weeks unemployed job searching
Leave school 17-18

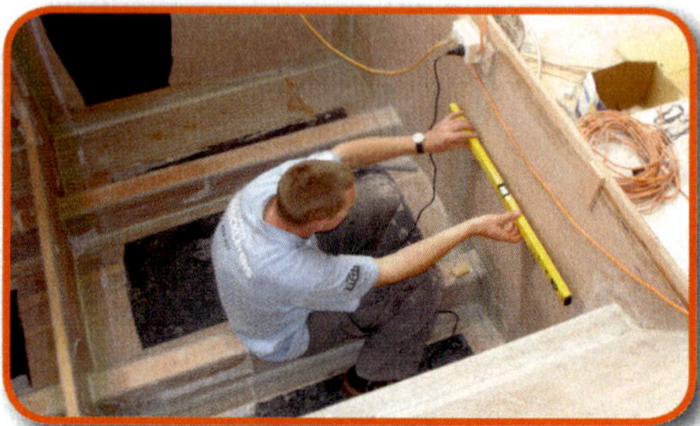

Of course this won't be the pattern for everyone. A few young people go straight into jobs. Others get an apprenticeship. But the average length of time in one job is only 3-4 years now! School leavers can expect to have about 6-10 jobs in their lifetimes. What's more they may often do totally different kinds of work in those jobs! The ups and downs of the spiral pattern is a reality for many!

Activities 18

1 Think about the two different patterns of working. Write down one good thing about each pattern. Now write down one thing about working in the past and in the present that might not be so good.

2 Below are five muddled words (all found on this page). See how fast you can solve them:

a **Rokw**
b **Ytpeolhc**
c **Rislap**
d **Itnra**
e **Tpetnar**

For those of you who have got those five, try this one:
Pepactrpiihens

(Clue: it has to do with d) above)

Working in a full-time job is still the most common way of doing paid work. Things are changing quite quickly though. More and more people are working in a wider variety of ways. Look at the Past and Present boxes below:

	PAST	PRESENT
1	Most people working in one or two permanent, long-lasting jobs.	Most people changing jobs at least 6-10 times during their lives.
2	Most working full-time.	More people working part-time or in temporary or seasonal jobs. Some work in two or three jobs at the same time.
3	Most working between 8am and 5pm on weekdays only.	Large numbers working on shifts – at night, in the early morning or in weekends.
4	Most working on farms or in factories or shops.	About 70% of people working in areas like education, health, tourism, business services or information technology.
5	Most employed by others in big firms, or as farmers on small farms.	Many more working in small firms. Also many more working for themselves, often on their own. Many work from home offices.
6	Hardly any people unemployed.	More people having short periods of unemployment between jobs or between periods of training.
7	Most training only once in their lives, before starting work or on the job.	More getting higher qualifications after school, then re-training off and on through their lives.

Activities 19

1 There are seven Work Trends in the chart above. Using the Present list, match each one with one of the people described in the A-G boxes. For example **3** and **D** - **Matthew** (not the correct match!)

2 Give an example of someone else working in one of the Present ways. It could be a friend or family member. Or you could do some Internet research using phrases like 'home office', 'self-employed', 'shift work', 'seasonal jobs' and so on.

A

Kate had 20 minutes to get to her Tourism Management course at polytech. She was in her last year of a three year Diploma course. Today was a long day. She'd just finished four hours on the supermarket check-out. After her two hour lecture she had to come back and do three more hours. She worked 25 hours a week to help pay her study fees. She hoped to get a job next year in tourism. Work as a Hotel Manager was her goal.

B

Kelly was feeling a bit depressed. It was the second time she had lost her job in the last six years. Part of the problem was she hadn't worked too hard at school. She had tried to get a hairdressing apprenticeship but couldn't find one. Her first job in a little jewellery shop was quite fun but the owner went out of business and that was that. After three weeks she'd found a job in a gift shop. Better money too. Then she'd got sick and after lots of time off she'd had to quit. Now she was well again but at a loose end. She knew she needed some training. Perhaps she'd go to the local polytechnic and see what they could suggest.

C

James enjoys moving round the country picking up short-term orchard jobs. Sometimes he picks or prunes kiwifruit in the Bay of Plenty for three or four months. Then he might go down to Otago to pick apricots. Sometimes he does two jobs like picking in the morning and serving in a takeaway shop in the evenings. He needs a reliable car to get to his jobs. He has saved some money and hopes to do a horticulture training course soon.

D

When **Matthew** left school he joined up with a fishing boat as a deckhand. He had always loved fishing. After two years he had had enough of this so looked for something different. He liked the idea of being an auctioneer. He was employed as a trainee, and worked at this for over a year. He liked the business of selling things so he joined a real estate firm to sell houses. He did well at this over many years. Then he began to look around again.

E

Sarah had done a Food Technology degree after leaving school. Then she had worked in a big firm researching new kinds of dairy foods. She enjoyed it and wanted to help recruit and train others. She decided she would do a one year course at university called Human Resource Management. After that she became involved in selecting new workers for her firm and training them. In a few years she hoped to do a business qualification too.

F

Tricia and **Mike Legg** run a huge business from their home office in Paeroa. After teaching for some years Tricia decided to use her skills in floral design. She was also fascinated by the Internet and developing websites. She put the two together and now on their website they run training sessions and sell DVDs and CDs that they make about floral design. They also publish a print magazine which goes all round the world. They have over 5000 subscribers world-wide. The best thing is they love working from home and if they want to go for a swim at 2 o'clock on a hot day they can!

G

Hone worked in a plastics factory. He had to wear protective clothes. He also wore ear-muffs because of the noise. He was a supervisor and had a team of six people managing the big machines that made plastic cling-wrap. Usually he worked from 10pm to 6am. Sometimes though the roster changed and he worked during the day instead. He preferred the night shift because after a sleep in the morning he had some of the afternoon free.

The kinds of jobs we work at have changed a lot over recent years. So have the hours we work and the qualifications we need. The facts and figures below show some of these changes.

Resource 1

Changing Roles for Men and Women

	1975		2005	
	Women	Men	Women	Men
Members of Parliament	5%	95%	29%	71%
Mayors of towns, citites	0.7%	99.3%	19%	81%
School Principals	8%	92%	40%	60%
Average pay per hour	$2.07	$2.75	$18.89	$21.89

The box above shows how women especially have taken on new kinds of jobs. It also shows that, over all jobs, women earn less than men do. That was what happened in earlier years and it can still happen today. In June 2007, women earned 87.9% of what men earned per hour. Partly this is because women work more in clerical or shop jobs that don't pay as much as many of the jobs men do.

Resource 2

AGE AND UNEMPLOYMENT

Unfortunately there are many more young people who can't find jobs than older people:

In 2005, 13% of school leavers aged 15-19 were unemployed, while only 2% of people aged 60-64 were unemployed. School leavers with few qualifications were worst off. School qualifications are a help. Those with school qualifications plus polytechnic, apprenticeship, university or other after-school training were much more likely to find jobs.

Farming has always been important in New Zealand. But the ways we use our land are changing.

Resource 3

LAND USE

Going Up

- three or four small farms combining into one big farm
- more deer farms
- more horticulture, especially vines for making wine
- more small lifestyle blocks

Going Down

- number of farms overall
- fewer sheep and cattle farms
- fewer small dairy farms

The industries we work in have been changing too. Look at the graph below showing the change from 1996 to 2001.

Resource 4

INDUSTRY OF EMPLOYED POPULATION, 1996-2001

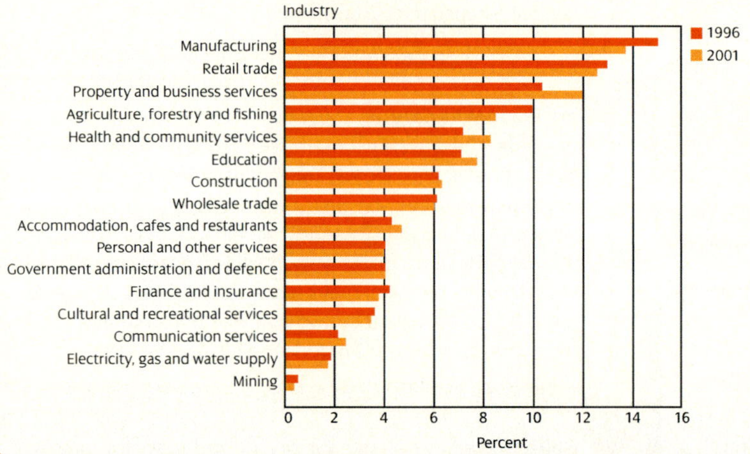

Industry

Manufacturing
Retail trade
Property and business services
Agriculture, forestry and fishing
Health and community services
Education
Construction
Wholesale trade
Accommodation, cafes and restaurants
Personal and other services
Government administration and defence
Finance and insurance
Cultural and recreational services
Communication services
Electricity, gas and water supply
Mining

1996
2001

0 2 4 6 8 10 12 14 16

Percent

Most people work full-time in their jobs. Bit by bit though more and more people are starting to work part-time instead. Some may have two or three part-time jobs at once.

1985 – 16.6% of people worked part-time
2001 – 22.7% of people worked part-time

Activities 20

1. Look at the three groups of people mentioned in Resource 1 above. Which group shows the biggest percentage change for women between 1975 and 2005?
2. Read Resource 2 again. What is one important reason for so many 15-19 year olds being unemployed?
3. Do some research on the wine industry and prepare a poster on it. Try to answer these questions in the poster:
   - **a** What is an oenologist?
   - **b** What regions of New Zealand are the most important for growing grape vines and making wine? Why?
   - **c** What other jobs are involved in the wine industry?
4. Check out the graph in Resource 4.
   - **a** What four industries have changed the most between 1996 and 2001?
   - **b** What 3 industries have had the biggest drops in the numbers they employ between 1996 and 2001?
   - **c** Can you re-draw this graph in another way?
   - **d** See if you can find a graph showing recent industries that people worked in.
5. Why do you think more people work part-time now? (Clues: hours of work, service industries, women)

8 Expanding Industries

Expanding Jobs

This chapter is about jobs that are not only changing but expanding. That is, the numbers of them are increasing. Some of these jobs are common or well-known jobs, like nurses and carpenters. Others, however, are jobs you may not have heard of at all!

An 'industry' is a whole big group of jobs that focus on the same kind of work. For example, the travel industry, which includes jobs like travel agents, tourist guides and airline pilots. Two industries that offered more jobs than most other industries between 2001 and 2006 were:

- business services, and
- personal services.

Hundreds of different jobs come into these two industries. In business services, for example: web-designers, marketing assistants or computer servicers. Personal services could include jobs like hairdressing, window cleaning or gardening.

One area where jobs are both growing and changing is the trades. Look at the diagram below which shows a few of these:

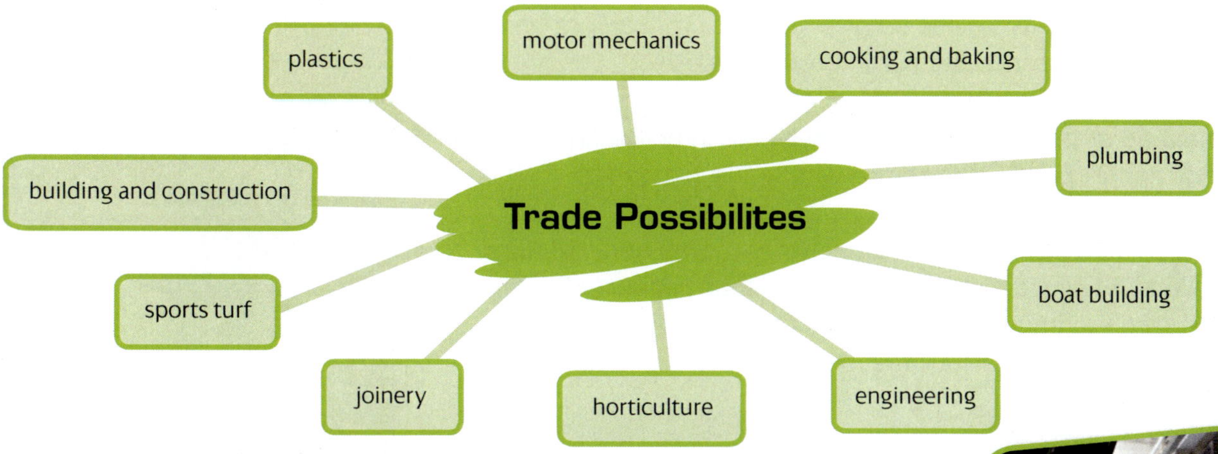

Trade Possibilites

- plastics
- motor mechanics
- cooking and baking
- plumbing
- building and construction
- boat building
- sports turf
- joinery
- horticulture
- engineering

Activities 21

1 Two industries grew especially fast between 2001 – 2006. Find them, and think of five jobs in each industry that are **not** mentioned above.

2 Apprentices and trade trainees study National Certificates just as you do, as well as training on the job. Do a web search, using words and phrases like trades, apprentices, Department of Labour etc. Choose one kind of training and find out what National Certificates they do, how long it might take and what school qualifications you need to have.

And there are many, many more. On top of that each trade has lots of different kinds of work within it. In engineering, for example, you can train to do aeronautical, fitting and turning or electrical trades, as well as others. Horticulture covers training in orchards, flowers or vegetables, and as a baker you could learn to make cakes and breads, or even tempting little pastries! What's even better, in many of these jobs you can earn very high wages. In 2004, for example, plumbers employed by others were earning $60,000 - $70,000 a year. If they were managers or self-employed they earned much more than that.

New technology is changing some of the trades in big ways. A motor mechanic used to learn how to fix a mostly mechanical engine. Now they must learn to understand and operate all kinds of new systems, often computer controlled, like the fuel system or the electrical system.

The lathe used for turning in the engineering workshop has now given way to expensive computer-controlled machines. And in the security industry electronic circuits now make up often quite complicated alarm systems of factories, offices and homes.

The tourism industry too is expanding and changing. It is expanding because more and more tourists are coming to visit. The changing part comes about, however, mainly because more visitors want to see and experience different kinds of things. They want different kinds of adventures and food, and they want to be shown **authentic** Maori culture. Also they expect top-class service, so tourism workers need to develop excellent personal and communication skills.

New kinds of tourism are emerging too. Sports tourism, for example, is aimed at people who visit to take part in or watch sport. Thousands of people came recently to watch the big yachts in the America's Cup competition.

Fashion, food and tourism are sometimes combined. Models showed off New Zealand-designed clothes in Japan recently. Special New Zealand food like paua fritters, and our top wines, were offered to guests. The aim was to encourage more Japanese people to visit our country.

Heard of These?

Lots of jobs exist that most of us know nothing about at all. Because of this employers often can't find enough people to do them. But some of these jobs are expanding quickly. They offer good training, interesting work and the possibility of earning very good wages. For example, what about a:

- flexo printer
- polymer scientist
- recycling technician.

All these people work in one particular industry. Think about people who may be making peanut butter containers, microwave dishes, garden hoses, freezer bags, CD cases and so on. By now you should have realised we're talking about the plastics industry. Plastics businesses make products and parts that you use each day. You probably don't think, though, about who designed or made them. It's a big industry and getting bigger. Four thousand new workers will be needed over the coming years!

Design in fact is another industry that is changing and expanding and isn't very well understood by people. Look at the diagram at the top of the next page:

Language Box

authentic: real, accurate.

Design Options

landscape
- gardens
- parks
- environmental
- sports grounds

creative
- photography
- painting
- fabric
- jewellery
- Maori craft
- visual arts

fashion
- accessories
- clothes
- children's wear

product
- chairs
- MP3 players
- toys

computer
- web design
- electronic modelling
- multi-media

graphic
- advertisements
- publishing
- DVD cases
- communication

spatial
- interior
- film/theatre
- architecture
- expos

And these are only some of the things that designers work at! Think about the shape of cars we'd like to own, or of the newest mobile phone, the cups in the kitchen or our bedroom furniture. Who designed the clothes or jewellery we wear, the web-sites we go to, the book covers in the library, the patterns on the curtains or the parks and gardens around us? The answer of course is one of thousands of creative people who have good ideas and the training to design them. Businesses always need designers to keep making or planning different things. Changing technology means designers have to continue changing too to keep up – and try to stay ahead of the opposition!

Some New Zealand designers do some really interesting jobs. It must be fun for example to design some of the weird creatures in movies like *Lord of the Rings* or *King Kong*. Many of you will have noticed too how the graphics have changed from time to time on our TV weather reports. New Zealand's MetService has a company called Metra which is considered so good it was asked to do all the weather graphics for the BBC – the British broadcasting service.

1 Choose one of the plastics industry jobs named on page 28 and do some research on it. Present your findings in a paragraph or a graphic form.

2 This page briefly describes the plastic and design industries. Two or three main points are being made about them. In groups of four, discuss these and answer the following questions:
   - **a** What are two of these main points?
   - **b** Why does it matter that you understand these points?

One of the biggest developing areas of work is Maori-owned and run businesses. Often people don't know much about these. In fact, in the 1980s and early 1990s many Maori – about 25,000 – became unemployed in New Zealand's economic **restructuring.** Like Pakeha people, though, many more of them are now employed in service industries. Look at the two graphs below:

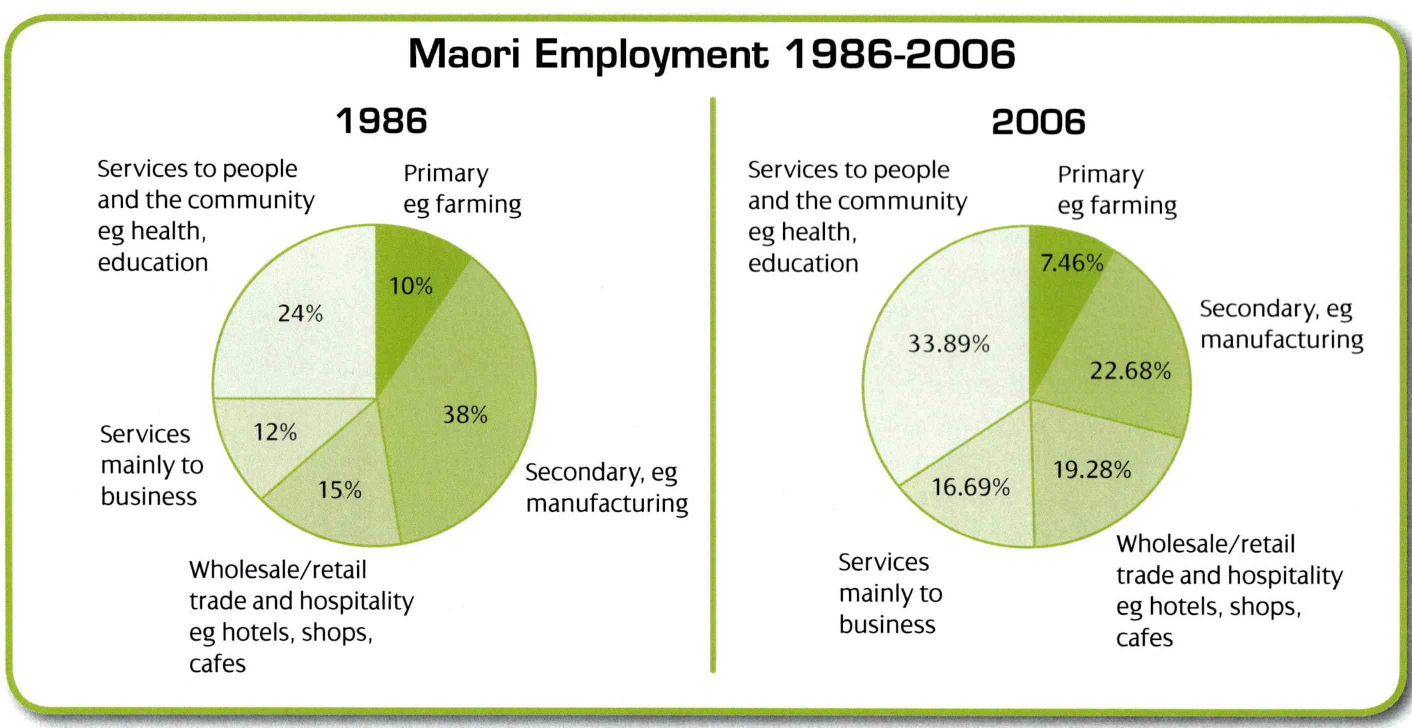

As well as changing the kind of work many of them did as employees, a large number of Maori became **entrepreneurs.** Many started setting up and running their own small businesses. A lot realised the big demand from overseas tourists for unique Maori cultural experiences. Some began marae stays with the local people welcoming, feeding and entertaining them, and explaining a little about the significance of their marae and history.

Others began guided tours or walks. Ngati Whatua in Auckland began Tamaki Hikoi for example, taking visitors on guided tours around sacred Maori landmarks in the city, including Mt Eden.

One of the most popular tourist visits is the Footprints Waipoua guided walks. Manager Koro Carmen says Maori guides take visitors through the Waipoua Forest in Northland, talking about the **ecology** and visiting the famous giant kauri trees. They also discuss Maori legends and stories, for example about the kiwi. Visitors love their four-hour night walk because they can hear and feel the forest around them, even if it is a bit eerie!

Koro Carmen in Waipoua Forest

Tamaki Maori Village

And in Rotorua and Christchurch, brothers Doug and Mike Tamaki have re-created Maori villages. Traditional welcomes and hangi are part of the experience, and sometimes tribal battles. Tourists see what happened when Pakeha brought diseases like the flu, and other events in New Zealand history.

There are also some huge Maori Trusts like the Wakatu Incorporation on the East Coast, employing hundreds of people in forestry, horticulture, and other businesses. Tohu Wines was begun by them. Tohu grow grapes in Marlborough, Nelson and Gisborne and sell about 90% of it overseas as a Maori wine. And of course Ngai Tahu in the South Island are expanding quickly. Besides all kinds of other businesses, they run big tourist adventures like the Shotover Jet Boats. They also established Whale Watch Kaikoura which is probably one of New Zealand's best-known tourism attractions, and they have big fishing businesses too.

Charles Royal of Rotorua is another who has begun what is today an expanding business. A chef, Charles also has a huge knowledge of bush herbs and spices that were used by early Maori. His Kinaki Wild Herbs are used by restaurants throughout New Zealand. They are also being exported.

Charles Royal

Whale Watch Kaikoura

Maori women especially have been getting all kinds of small businesses going. Wendy Bennett, for example, began a catering business in Auckland called Food Queens. This supplied business lunches with a wide range of food including things like roasted Maori potatoes, or smoked pipi and kina. Now she runs **Indigenous** Food tours from Gisborne, providing New Zealand food and hospitality in Maori homes.

Others from New Zealand's many ethnic groups are setting up exciting new small businesses too. Indian, Thai, Turkish and Korean cafés and restaurants are examples. Crafts of all kinds, market stalls, IT businesses or newsletters for immigrants in their own languages are all providing new jobs.

Language Box

restructuring: to change something around; part of this restructuring was to sell government-owned departments like the railways, or to reduce the numbers employed. Large numbers of Maori worked in these departments and many lost their jobs.

entrepreneurs: people who think up very new ideas to make into a small business.

ecology: studying the influence plants and animals have on each other and on their environments.

indigenous: native to a country.

Activities 23

1 Look at the pie graphs showing Maori employed by others.
   - **a** What are the two biggest areas of change from 1986 to 2006? How have they changed?
   - **b** Why was government restructuring in the 1980s a big problem for many Maori?

2 In 2005 there were over 600 Maori-owned tourism businesses in New Zealand. Use the Internet, Yellow Pages or other means to choose one from your local area. Find out what it offers, how many people run it and any other information you can. Present your findings in a poster or other graphic form.

9 Future Work

As we saw in Chapter 8, there are many traditional industries that have been expanding. Some of these, such as tourism, will keep on growing. Teachers of all kinds will be needed. So will the huge range of health jobs, including caring for old people at home. Personal services like hairdressing and gardening will be in demand. So will trades jobs. Business jobs like accounting and banking will be available, though they may be different from how they are today. And of course recreation, sport and entertainment will provide lots of interesting work.

Many future jobs though haven't been invented yet. This is especially so in some of the areas in the 'Tomorrow's Jobs' diagram below. All we can do is name the general areas where jobs are likely to be. Many of these will be explained more in the next two pages.

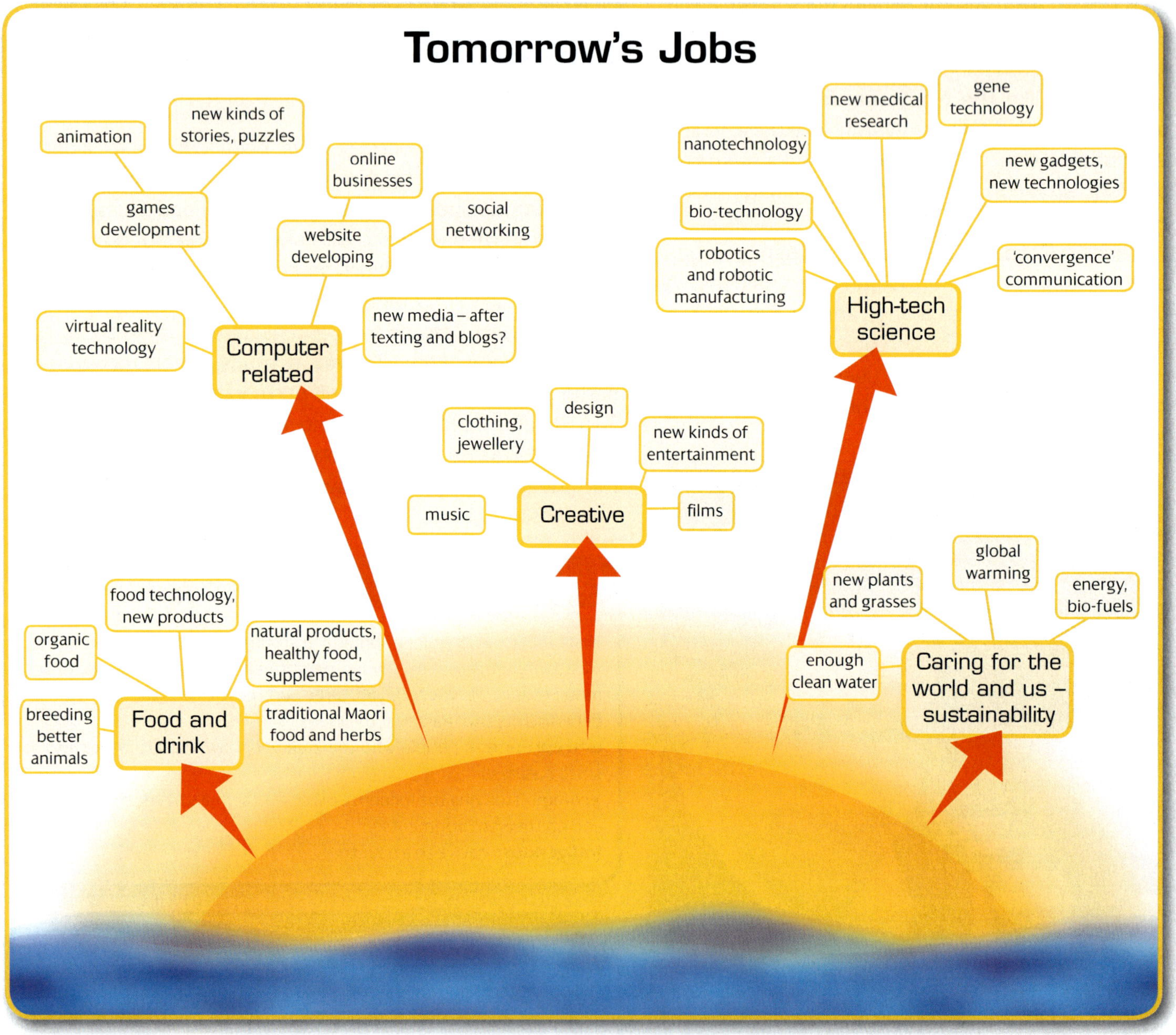

Tomorrow's Jobs

Computer related
animation
new kinds of stories, puzzles
games development
online businesses
social networking
website developing
virtual reality technology
new media – after texting and blogs?

High-tech science
new medical research
gene technology
nanotechnology
new gadgets, new technologies
bio-technology
robotics and robotic manufacturing
'convergence' communication

Creative
clothing, jewellery
design
new kinds of entertainment
music
films

Food and drink
food technology, new products
organic food
natural products, healthy food, supplements
breeding better animals
traditional Maori food and herbs

Caring for the world and us – sustainability
global warming
new plants and grasses
energy, bio-fuels
enough clean water

Activities 24

1 Name five of the traditional industries likely to provide jobs in the future.

2 These two words written in code will be important in the future. Use the code buster below to solve them.
5 7 4 8 9 6 1 10 5 8 7
2 9 3 1 10 5 11 5 10 12

Codebuster:
12-y, 11-v, 10-t, 9-r, 8-o, 7-n, 6-m, 5-i, 4-f, 3-e, 2-c, 1-a.

3 Look at the five main groups of tomorrow's jobs in the diagram. Now think about the kinds of jobs leading from them. Name three school subjects that are going to be important to several of these job areas.

The good *health* of people, animals, farms and the environment will encourage a big range of future jobs. People want to stay healthy and prevent illness. They are worried about toxic chemicals in the environment. The health of our water, air and animals is becoming more and more important. New Zealand produces lots of food, and people we export to insist that it is produced safely and more naturally. The diagram below shows some of the areas that will produce new jobs:

Health

organic
native plants
natural
biotechnology 'healthy' foods
vitamin/mineral supplements

climate change
'green' business
sustainability
biofuels
recycling
new energy source
ecology
clean water
agricultural research

Biotechnology and food technology scientists work to develop extra healthy foods. Many are called 'functional foods', that is, they have added vitamins or minerals. Fonterra for example adds extra calcium to milk. Tatua Dairy Company makes protein ingredients which they export to companies to put in sports drinks or baby foods. Other companies make products from natural things like wool, or drugs for human health problems.

Natural and organic products are becoming more popular. Partly this is because of nasty food scares like 'mad cow' disease. Also some people would rather use natural or herbal products than antibiotics or other chemical drugs. N.Z. companies produce things like mussel supplements, manuka honey or deer velvet products, and herbal skincare. Native plants like pikopiko and horopito are being used for foods and for improving our health. Many science and manufacturing jobs are involved.

We have to find new kinds of ***energy***. Petrol is very expensive in our cars, and so are electricity and gas in our homes. What's more, producing these things often adds to the world's greenhouse gases. We need **renewable** energy. We already make a lot renewably from hydro and geothermal power stations, but not enough. Researching and setting up better wind farms, solar power products and biofuels will need many more workers. Vegetable oils, dairy effluent, pinetrees and other things can be used to make bio-fuels.

If something is renewable, it is **sustainable**. That means it can keep on being used in future. People overseas want sustainable products. They want N.Z.'s fish as long as we leave enough alive to breed more for future generations. Tourists want to see our mountains, rivers and bush as long as those attractions stay looking untouched. That means we can't have too many people tramping everywhere or leaving rubbish behind! Solving puzzles like these will provide lots more jobs in future.

Water will be in short supply in future because of ***climate change***. We need to save water and use it better. Also agricultural scientists are experimenting with plants that will cope better with dry farmland. New grasses are also being developed that will stop cows and sheep producing so much gas! About half of N.Z.'s greenhouse gases are produced by farm animals. There will be more future jobs in things like these.

Many ***'green' businesses*** have started up. Many more will do so in the coming years. Examples are:

- the Taupo Prawn Farm which uses waste water from the Wairakei Power Station to heat the prawn breeding ponds.
- plastics manufacturing businesses are recycling more plastic every year.
- eco-tourism companies get tourists to help them in conservation efforts, e.g. trapping stoats to protect endangered birds or pulling out wild pine trees in the bush. Tourists enjoy feeling they are helping preserve the environment.
- sustainable buildings are being built, e.g. at the Papamoa Public Library windows open and close automatically to control the temperature and solar panels provide hot water. People who can design things like these will be in demand.

Activities 25

1 How is agriculture connected with people's health? Discuss in class.

2 Imagine your class is a team of medical researchers and biotechnologists. You have just worked out how to make people live for another 50 years. This is good news in one way but there will be problems. Should the team publicise the research or destroy it? As a class, discuss the implications of both choices, work out a process to make a decision, and then make it!

3 Choose *one* topic from the diagram on page 33. Do some research on it. What are its benefits? Problems? Present your findings in a five minute speech to the class.

Language Box

renewable: able to be used again and again.
sustainable: something that can be used now and in the future.

No one can really predict what will happen in the future. There are some trends now, however, that over the next 5-10 years seem likely to produce new jobs.

Two words describe a large number of these new jobs:

- high tech
- creative.

Some jobs will cover both these aspects. Jobs in **nanotechnology**, robotic research or computer games development, for example, will certainly need high-tech science, computer or engineering skills. But they will also need people with lots of creativity and imagination who can think up new possibilities or see new patterns and trends.

Some jobs might need people who have a very good knowledge of mainly technical things. A word called 'convergence' is being used a lot now. It means bringing together in one gadget or piece of equipment different things like the Internet, TV and phone. Or maybe devising a cellphone that gets the Internet and email, screens videos, takes photos, has a GPS receiver, acts as a game-playing machine and turns on the heaters in your house before you arrive home! Good keyboard and technology skills will be essential in fitting all this together in one small device.

Other future jobs will need many of the talents we treasure today. Creative musicians, story-tellers, actors and film-makers, graphic, jewellery and fashion designers, animation programers, visual artists and so on will always be needed.

Look at these trends in the high-tech area. You may already be a part of some of them:

Language Box

nanotechnology: engineering at a molecular level; manipulating clusters of atoms to make tiny things. Mix of physics, chemistry and biology.
replicating: copying, in this case reproducing themselves.

- More people are already involved worldwide in developing computer games than in film-making. This trend is likely to increase. Very good computer skills are needed, with training in programing.
- More and more people want to download, watch or listen to TV shows, movies or music they personally like, and they want to do so at a time they choose themselves.
- Nanotechnology and other technologies are being used to produce machines that are self-**replicating**. This means that a 'nanofactory' could make tiny machines you can't even see that will produce thousands more tiny machines all by themselves! No people needed! They will be able to make any machine that has been designed on a computer.
- More 'intelligent' machines are being produced. Some robots are beginning to be able to mimic or copy the human brain in simple ways. They will become more and more clever over coming years.
- More people are using the Internet to socialise and network with other people e.g. on sites like Bebo and My Space. Some people would prefer to do this rather than meet people face to face.
- More and more small businesses exist only on the Internet. It is often a good way for people who can do unusual things to 'make a job' for themselves, and perhaps others. For example, a juggler who wants to sell juggling equipment he makes, or a person who collects old vinyl records and wants to sell or trade them.
- New medical research is finding that gene technology can do amazing things. New organs like kidneys, for example, may be able to be grown from stem cells in someone's body. Decisions about whether it's all right to choose the sex of a baby or clone a person may have to be made in the next few years.

Activities 26

1 Several high-tech areas are likely to create future jobs. One or two of those mentioned above, however, could mean that jobs are lost. Name one of these.

2 Use this page and the 'Tomorrow's Jobs' diagram on page 32 to make up at least five multi-choice questions to add to a class quiz.

3 Think about how people, including your friends, are using the Internet now. What two or three trends or patterns do you think are developing? What do you think could be the results of these in five years?
Express your answers graphically or in words. Then in groups of four discuss these and come up with a summary of your main findings.

Preparing for Future Work

If you have read some of the other chapters you will be beginning to understand how quickly jobs and the ways we do them are changing. You may be wondering though what it all means for you. Look again at some of the areas where jobs will be expanding:

The good news is that you are *already* planning for your future jobs. Look at the lists of skills, personal qualities and so on below. Think about what you already have, and what you're learning through your subjects and other activities.

Skills Example

What are skills? How do you know you have them?
Well, if you:-

- have an ability in...
- show a talent for...
- have learnt to do well in...
- have a gift for...
- show an instinct for...
- are good at...

...something, and you do it reasonably well, then you probably have a 'skill' in that area. In other words, a skill is something you show you can do well.

Skills List

- cook a nutritious meal
- use tools to make something
- budget pocket money or wages carefully
- play in a sports team
- look after young children
- calculate measurements accurately
- design attractive posters, pictures or clothes
- play a musical instrument
- speak two or more languages
- use a computer program well
- write accurate descriptions of things you see or do
- grow seeds or plants
- speak confidently to a group
- read books easily
- organise all the details for a big event.

Personal Qualities

- willing to work hard
- open to trying new things, being flexible
- respecting other cultures
- caring for friends, family and workmates who have problems
- honesty
- being curious
- being self-disciplined

And again there are many, many more qualities you probably have that will help you enormously in your future jobs.

Activities 27

1 Read the Skills Example and Skills List again. Make your own list of 5-10 skills that **you** have. Don't forget to add any that are not on this list. Along with understanding your skills, you need to know all about the job you're interested in. So, get ready to make some tough decisions. Get into groups of four. One pair of you will present a good case for choosing a career in **a** below. The other pair will do the same for **b**.
The two alternatives:

a tourist guide **or** journalist
b plastics designer **or** electrician.

At this stage we are presuming you have the right school subjects and qualifications to do any of these jobs. Do some research first – on the Internet or in the careers room. You will be arguing for your chosen career on the basis of: what kind of training you need and whether you or the employer will pay for it, the wages, hours of work, job prospects, amount of stress involved and so on.

Each pair should then present their case to the other pair. You may want to follow this with a class discussion.

There is something else you need to know about. Some of the most important job-preparation you can do involves understanding 'transferable skills.' These are skills you can use in all sorts of different jobs and situations. For example if you can speak or understand another language like Spanish or Chinese, you could use it to teach, to translate for others, to use on a tourist bus, to arrange a business deal in another country, or to talk to foreign friends.

There are three main kinds of transferable skills. Here are some examples of them:

1 Work Skills

- being punctual, finishing tasks on time,
- adapting quickly to new situations or places,
- being keen to learn new things,
- understanding the difference between play and work, e.g. not playing fun computer games at work,
- being able to 'multi-task', that is managing two or three tasks at once,
- doing a part-time job or volunteer work while studying,
- listening carefully and following orders,
- problem-solving, using mind maps or other methods to do so,
- being able to be inventive or develop creative ideas when asked to.

2 Communication Skills

- getting on well with work-mates of all ages and races,
- sharing knowledge and tasks when working in teams,
- developing relationships with people working at a distance e.g. by phone or email, and doing what you say you'll do.

3 Technological Skills

- being competent with a variety of computer programs and functions,
- understanding how other technology works, e.g. video cameras, sound recording equipment, Internet, multi-media, CAD/CAM and so on,
- understanding things like confidentiality when using new technology.

Out of school interests often turn into jobs.

Innovation and creativity are important.

The boundaries of time and space are disappearing with new technology – we can work anytime, anywhere!

Technology, design, language and other skills learnt at school give good preparation for later.

Core subjects like English, Maths and Sciences are very important – don't drop them all to take more 'interesting' or 'exciting' subjects!

Activities 28

1 Name five transferable skills you think you have. Friends or family can often help you name these. Now name two you haven't got that you want to work on this year.

2 Some clever person thought up the terms 'digital natives' and 'digital immigrants'. You are probably a digital native; that is you were brought up with TVs, computers and so on. Your parents and other older people are more likely to be digital immigrants though. That is they were brought up with books, radios and maybe early TVs. They've had to learn how to operate new technology but it might still be a bit foreign at times! That is, they are kind of 'immigrating' into a new way of working. One day you might be a digital immigrant into new forms of technology not yet developed! Discuss this in class.

Snakes and Ladders

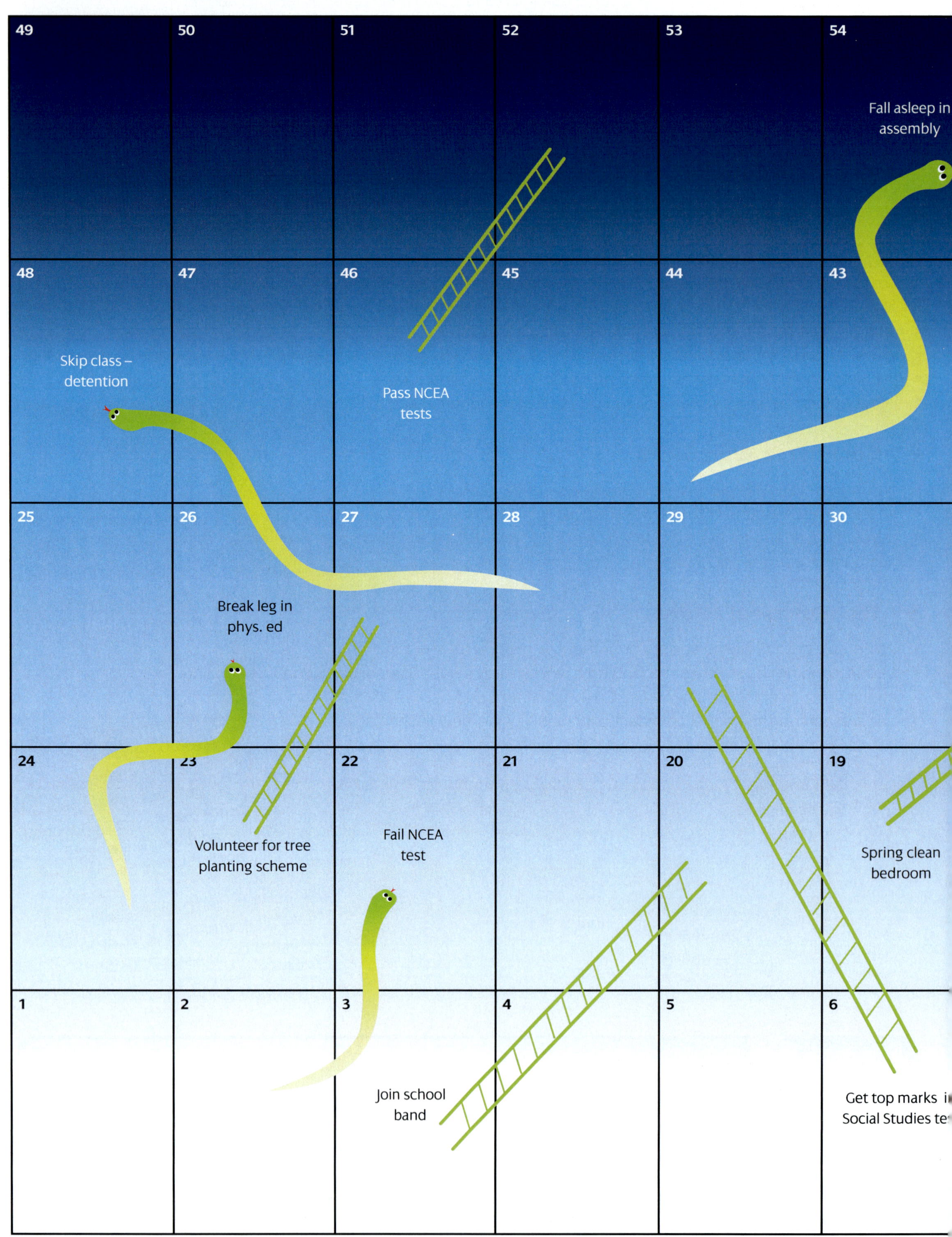

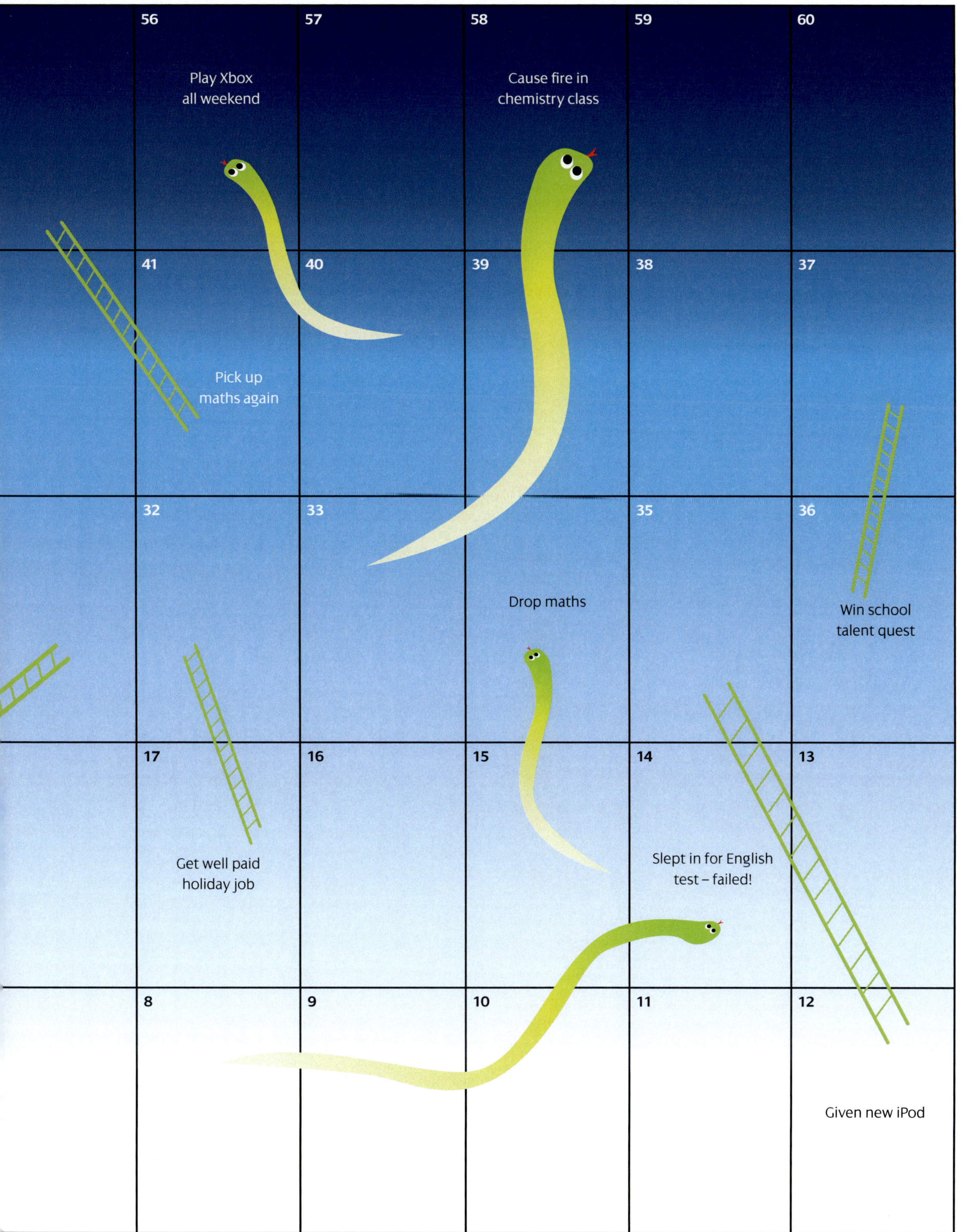
56
Play Xbox
all weekend
57
58
Cause fire in
chemistry class
59
60
41
Pick up
maths again
40
39
38
37
32
33
35
Drop maths
36
Win school
talent quest
17
Get well paid
holiday job
16
15
14
Slept in for English
test – failed!
13
8
9
10
11
12
Given new iPod